U. MILO KAUFMANN

Paradise
in the Age of Milton

EIS
EDITIONS

ELS Editions
Department of English
University of Victoria
Victoria, BC
Canada V8W 3W1
www.elseditions.com

Founding Editor: Samuel L. Macey

General Editor: Luke Carson

Printed by CreateSpace

English literary studies monograph series
ISSN 0829-7681 ; 11
ISBN-10 0-920604-20-X
ISBN-13 978-0-920604-20-5

CONTENTS

Introduction   7

CHAPTER ONE.   Milton and the Versions of Paradise   11

   1.1   Finitude Manqué   12

   1.2   The Heavenly Life   16

   1.3   Earth's Marriage   23

CHAPTER TWO.   Paradise and Miltonic Theodicy   34

   2.1   Moral and Aesthetic Theodicies   34

   2.2   Milton's Cosmic Meliorism   39

CHAPTER THREE.   Herrick and Marvell: The Paradisal Quest   51

   3.1   Herrick and the Search for Secure Space   51

   3.2   Dialectic and Pilgrimage   57

   3.3   Transcendence and Marvell's Green World   68

Notes   76

ACKNOWLEDGMENTS

Many of the matters examined here benefitted richly, when they were no more than speculations, from discussions with my former office-mate Patrick Grant. In all stages important contributions have come from my students at the University of Illinois, Urbana-Champaign. I lament that that debt is too diffuse, too long a-building, for me to document as I would like. One former student, James Obertino, has read the manuscript and provided much useful criticism.

An earlier version of Chapter One I gave as a lecture for the Department of English at the University of Victoria in the fall of 1974. The inspiration of that occasion was, I am sure, the major encouragement in my organizing these materials for a larger audience.

Finally I honor my wife, Helen Olson Kaufmann, for fixing in the world around her so many of the felicities I discuss below.

INTRODUCTION

In her recent study of the history of utopias,[1] Ms. Elisabeth Hansot demonstrates that the seventeenth century encompassed a major transition in how utopias were presented in the West. Before 1600 they were more or less free of process and imperfection. After 1700 utopias tended to be goals to be achieved in history, and of necessity incorporated change and conflict. The Greek predilection for associating ideal reality with products and states was yielding to an Hebraic identification of the ideal with historical process.

Though I am concerned here not with utopias but with paradise—that is, not with model societies, but with those literary and scriptural constructions which feature the interpenetration of earth and heaven—I find Ms. Hansot's summary a significant parallel to the development I am discussing. In the portraying of paradise, the Age of Milton describes a shift from static pastoral enclaves to images of joyful career and idealized process. Felicity comes to be inseparable from openness and change.

We know that earthly geography in the 17th century ceased to be a domain capable of incorporating even while concealing the lost Eden. In 1617 John Salkeld, chaplain to James I, could say:

> ... if Paradise were not a reall and corporall place, how could there flow out of it those foure rivers, which (as the Scripture witnesseth) compasse the whole earth? How should *Enoch* and *Elias* be translated thither, and (as many writers affirme) be conserved there both in body and soule? Yea, otherwise how should *Adam* and *Eve* have lived there?[2]

But while these rhetorical questions imply that the paradisal garden must indeed be yet extant, Salkeld could not have assumed general agreement on the point among his contemporaries.[3] The voyages of discovery were dissolving the bond between geographical remoteness and the mysteries of Paradise. And Milton, if we may judge from his final disposition of the Garden in Noah's Flood, completely accepts the new perspective. Here is Michael's description to Adam of Eden's fate:

> ... all the Cataracts
> Of Heav'n set open on the Earth shall pour
> Rain day and night, all fountains of the Deep

7

> Broke up, shall heave the Ocean to usurp
> Beyond all bounds, till inundation rise
> Above the highest Hills: then shall this Mount
> Of Paradise by might of Waves be mov'd
> Out of his place, push'd by the horned flood,
> With all his verdure spoil'd, and Trees adrift
> Down the great River to the op'ning Gulf,
> And there take root an Island salt and bare,
> The haunt of Seals and Orcs, and Sea-mews' clang.

If the implications of this transformation of walled garden to desert island were not apparent enough, the poet adds that this is

> To teach thee that God attributes to place
> *No sanctity, if none be thither brought*
> *By Men who there frequent,* or therein dwell.[4] (Italics added)

Such a dissociation of sacred mystery from place had, we recall, notable and diverse expressions in Milton's century. In religion the dissenters were working out the implications of Calvin's dictum that the church exists wherever the Word is preached and the sacraments of baptism and holy communion are administered. In politics, 1649 saw the Lord's anointed temple, in the shape of Charles' perfumed and handsome head, condemned to the block by Judges Goffe, Whalley and Dixwell. Anglican poet George Herbert was perfecting a slim volume of exquisite lyrics which offered to show that the Temple was now to be found in the well-ordered career of the obedient life.

In this secularization of space and relocation of the holy, it was not only religious war, the telescope, and the settling of the New World that proved decisive. Descartes' analytical geometry carried the mathematization of space and location to new levels of abstractness, even as the new physics of Galileo and Newton firmly fixed in human consciousness the spectral cartoons of colorless masses negotiating in the void.

To suggest how the career of the island-haven is indeed a précis of this secularization, I note several images to be considered with the picture of Milton's Eden become a desert haunt of orcs and sea-mews. In the 1630's Andrew Marvell writes about the Bermudas, but his praise of that charmed haven is curiously hedged. A band of Puritans fleeing persecution approaches the islands in their ship's boat while singing this song:

> He lands us on a grassy Stage;
> Safe from the Storms, and Prelat's rage.
> He gave us this eternal Spring,
> Which here enamells every thing. . . . [5]

Our surrender to this island paradise—which the poet goes on to describe, typically, in terms of seductive fruit and noble trees—is frustrated by those tonal cues of "grassy *Stage*" (italics added) and the enamelled landscape. Plainly this is no Eden. The poem concludes,

> And all the way, to guide their Chime,
> With falling Oars they kept the time.

The vision of the islands turns out to be no more than a sea chantey, a song sung to keep up spirits while the oars are plied.

By 1719, a mere century after Salkeld's work, when Defoe publishes his account of Crusoe's island, the paradisal island has become thoroughly profaned. Crusoe's island is secular space, *par excellence*; and in Defoe's later presentation of Robert Drury's island, or Madagascar, we have not so much an interlude in a tropical Eden as fifteen years of struggle, marriage and childbearing that read distressingly like life in any fallen human community.

This sketch of the fate of Milton's Eden, a fate which paradisal enclaves as a class experienced in the 17th century, serves to introduce the three related studies which follow. In the first of these I suggest how the primordial garden is transcended in the Miltonic scheme by two other versions of paradise better able to accommodate process. In the second I relate the imaging of paradise to two kinds of Miltonic theodicy. The third study proposes complementary readings of Herrick and of Marvell which illustrate how in Milton's context the incorporation of process into the paradisal involves solutions corroborative of Milton's own. Herrick's *Noble Numbers* provide a redefining of the paradisal enclave, while Marvell's lyrics set forth a dialectical approach to pilgrimage in the green world. In these several cases the fundamental question being honored is that of how paradise comes to assimilate in Milton's age those qualities of openness traditionally identified with the abyss.

I mention now an assumption important to critical method in what follows. The readings of Milton, and indeed of all the poets I discuss, assume that imagery and narrative structures may, by the careful adducing of derivation (or other explanatory contexts), be shown to carry meanings beyond those provided by the narrator in expository fashion. It would not be necessary even to mention this, I suppose, were not the major figure in my argument a poet who seems to insist upon a readily accessible plain sense, with that plain sense one which has always encouraged theological rather than strictly literary apprehension. The scholarship upon Milton has long been divided over the issue of how to weigh the utterances of the epic voice in *Paradise Lost* whenever they appear to diverge from what the *mythos* of the poem—its story and imagery—suggest. I assume one is not free to mend that division merely by ignoring *mythos*, and take comfort in knowing that both medieval and modern hermeneutics recognize the category of the speaking object.

CHAPTER ONE

Milton and the Versions of Paradise

Milton's God, speaking in *Paradise Lost* shortly before his son moves out upon the Deep to inscribe the order of the cosmos with golden compasses, says that he

> in a moment will create
> Another world, out of one man a Race
> Of men innumerable, there to dwell,
> Not here, till by degrees of merit rais'd
> They open to themselves at length the way
> Up hither, under long obedience tri'd,
> And Earth be chang'd to Heav'n, and Heav'n to Earth,
> One Kingdom, Joy and Union without end.   (VII. 154-161)

Conspicuous in this forecast is God's promise of goods which transcend the paradise of Eden. Eden constitutes one version of the marriage of earth and heaven, but by no means the only one and plainly not even the best.

The entire drama of Fall and Redemption, moreover, receives no mention in this passage, nor does it need to. The progress of man beyond Eden appears to be a divine ordination for which man's lapse is a mere contingency. Indeed, it is difficult to see how a Fortunate Fall can be argued with any final serious-ness, since the beatific consummation foretold here holds true whether Eden is left in remorse or in delight.

Given such a far-reaching and ineluctable vision of felicity, what may we identify as the several specific versions of paradise which Milton is most concerned to set forth in *Paradise Lost*? I list three, each of which may be defined in terms of a characteristic strategy for relating fallen reality to ideal reality:[1]

> 1. The Paradisal Enclave
>   or Finitude Manqué;
> 2. The Paradisal Way
>   or Rectified Finitude;
> 3. The Final Marriage of Earth and Heaven
>   or Consummated Finitude.

Finitude manqué, in its prototypes, involves the imaging of earthly life before man's Fall and in the case of both sacred and secular artists assumes the descriptive strategy of subtracting from present reality everything regarded as evil. Rectified finitude involves the divine repair of the Fall for individuals in a regenerate and heavenly life. Consummated finitude involves a correction of the Fall for the whole of nature and the human community. In the writings of Milton and his contemporaries, both of the later versions involve a significant accommodation of process in the imaging of the ideal. The tradition of heavenly-mindedness stemming from John Calvin I shall argue to be a primary influence in the matter, though plainly that discussion must wait upon a proper examination of the first version, which was in Milton's age proving to be an inadequate vehicle of human aspiration.

1.1   Finitude Manqué

Finitude manqué is, I suppose, that version of paradise which literary artists have always found easiest to present. One subtracts from the plenum of ordinary reality the evils of pain, want, conflict, and death and presents the sublimed remainder. I think it just to call the result finitude manqué in view of how many values this approach sacrifices—in particular those of dynamics and openness. The typical representations of finitude manqué are recognizable as sanctuaries or hideaways existing in precarious tension with a larger, and more commodious world. Finitude manqué is often cast as a walled garden, or as an island like Sir Thomas More's or Aldous Huxley's. It may be a thinly disguised variant of the womb, or of childhood. It may indeed be a planet, or a whole unspoiled island galaxy, but the implications are always the same: finitude manqué is part of a larger order which threatens it.

Milton so describes his Garden of Eden:

> [I]n this pleasant soil
> His far more pleasant Garden God ordain'd;
> Out of the fertile ground he caus'd to grow
> All Trees of noblest kind for sight, smell, taste;
> And all amid them stood the Tree of Life,
> High eminent, blooming Ambrosial Fruit
> Of vegetable Gold; the next to Life
> Our Death the Tree of Knowledge grew fast by,
> Knowledge of Good bought dear by knowing ill.
>   . . .   Thus was this place,
> A happy rural seat of various view:
> Groves whose rich Trees wept odorous Gums and Balm,
> Others whose fruit burnisht with Golden Rind
> Hung amiable, *Hesperian* Fables true,
> If true, here only, and of delicious taste:
> Betwixt them Lawns, or level Downs, and Flocks

12

Grazing the tender herb, were interpos'd,
Or palmy hillock, or the flow'ry lap
Of some irriguous Valley spread her store,
Flow'rs of all hue, and without Thorn the Rose. . . .

(IV. 214-222, 246-256)

In this delectable pastoral landscape the two details which undoubtedly capture attention are those which involve an exclusion: the tree of moral knowledge, forbidden, which is also "our death"; and the rose free of thorns. If the forbidden tree is provocative for the way in which it poses the conscienceless innocence of Adam and Eve, the thornless rose is provocative for the way in which it poses the questions of the dynamics of nature in the Garden. Presumably the rose is thornless because thorns cause pain; and pain is ruled out of the paradise by definition, at least in the case of finitude manqué. Parallels to this feature of Milton's Eden are plentiful. Here, for example, is a description of the land of Dilmun taken from a Sumerian text dating from the 3rd millennium B.C.

> The land Dilmun is a pure place, the land Dilmun is a clean
> place,
> The land Dilmun is a clean place, the land Dilmun is a bright
> place;
> He who is all alone laid himself down in Dilmun.
> The place, after Enki had laid himself by his wife,
> That place is clean, that place is bright;
>
> . . .
>
> In Dilmun the raven uttered no cries,
> The *kite* uttered not the cry of the *kite*,
> The lion killed not,
> The wolf snatched not the lamb,
> Unknown was the kid-killing dog,
> Unknown was the grain-devouring *boar*,
>
> . . .
>
> The sick-eyed says not "I am sick-eyed,"
> The sick-headed says not "I am sick-headed,"
>
> . . .
>
> The singer utters no wail,
> By the side of the city he utters no lament.[2]

Does this exclusion of pain from paradise withstand scrutiny? Surely we must conclude that paradise is painless only at the expense of its being wholly anaesthetic, since pain is ordinarily the crossing of a threshold in the intensity of sensation. If there is to be feeling, there must be the possibility of pain. The only alternative is to have creatures who are so fully programmed that they will necessarily avoid all perilous contingencies.

What is true for pain must also be true for conflict and for want. If the lion is not eating meat, he is not eating at all, for he hasn't the herbivore's four stomachs to handle grass. While finitude manqué is the version of paradise most readily imaged, it is also the one most quickly seen through. For it to have any coherence whatsoever, it must be supposed to exist in a timeless moment. Like Sleeping Beauty's castle, the paradisal garden waits the human act which shall touch all to life.

Professor Helmut Klages, Professor of Sociology at the Technical University in Berlin, has recently compared the ideal societies literature offers with the real societies which sociology struggles to understand. The former characteristically slight the fact of external influence, of conflict and growth. In contrast,

1) Modern societies evidence a tendency towards permanent change.

2) Modern societies are complex in the highest degree; in fact, they develop through differentiation.

3) Modern societies show increasing contradictoriness.[3]

While one need not share Professor Klages' conviction that only the analysis of social reality itself offers any hope—and it is true that he is speaking of utopias rather than paradises—certainly he underlines the extreme vulnerability of finitude manqué. If it can be seen to incorporate change at all, it is change of a very low order.

I find it a mark both of Milton's courage and of his skill that he grasps the thistle as he does in presenting the daily milieu of unfallen Adam and Eve in the Garden. Scholarship, at least from the time of E. M. W. Tillyard, has debated the probability and coherence of the prelapsarian state in *Paradise Lost*, taking as a favorite gambit the question "When did Adam and Eve really fall?" but the most even-handed approach is to notice how deftly Milton integrates those features of finitude manqué upon which his sources insist—*viz.*, the absence of pain, want, and conflict in Eden—with a regime far more dramatic and dynamic than what is offered by any of the literary parallels.[4]

We see Adam and Eve at work, even if we cannot see how their work is vital to the ecological balance of the Garden. We see them learning, though we do not see how they have acquired the rudiments on which they build. In brief, we find Milton settling on paradox whenever he must to affirm both the givens of biblical tradition, and the dynamics of life in paradise. Though

14

he is subject, as he assures us in *Areopagitica* that every fallen human being is, to the curse of contraries, he yet undertakes to show us paradisal goods unqualified by attendant evil. Also, though paradise antedates history both individual and collective, Milton shows us characters who are both mature and knowledgeable. (Early commentators engaged this problem by proposing, among other novel solutions, that Adam was thirty years old at his creation, and was omniscient!)

It ought not to be imagined, however, that Milton's biblical sources contribute nothing to his vision but refractory elements like the supposed painlessness of Eden, and the "perfection" of its residents even before experience. The Genesis account of the Garden suggests that from the beginning its closed space was subject to two sorts of regular penetration from without, and each clearly implies a mode of transcendence which Milton does not hesitate to explore and amplify in the service of his own cosmic optimism.

The first penetration is by the Lord of the Garden, who comes there to talk with his rational creatures. Such conversation, we must suppose, would in Milton's scheme carry the clear promise of that ultimate Eden-transcending destiny which God describes at the time of the world's creation, and which Adam and Raphael discuss in *Paradise Lost*, Book V. The divine visitation—in the "cool" or freshening of evening, when the breeze moves through Eden and the human spirit is quickened—suggests, indeed, that whole order of transcendence by which the merely pastoral world is judged partial: God, heaven, moral structure, covenant, promise, law—in a word, the eternal *nomos* by which the world is straightened along the line of moral and spiritual growth. God's voice in Eden encapsulates that entire order of divine purpose later manifest in covenant and Incarnation which tugs man beyond the childhood of Eden. The Lord of the Garden is responsible for Adam's and Eve's vocation, the calling which in Milton's vision must eventually mean their mounting through all the worlds to God's side.

The second penetration is by the waters of the Deep, that abyssal reservoir which rose up in the Garden as mist or fountain, and which signified the intimate union between the closed space of Eden's enclave and the infinite possibilities of the abyss. The Garden of Eden, we are told in Genesis 2:10, was watered by a river which divided to make four tributaries. (Cf. *PL*, IV. 223 ff.) It had not yet rained, but a mist or flood rose up "from the earth and watered the whole face of the ground" (2:5-6). The note supplied in the *Oxford Annotated Bible* leads into a vast hinterland of significance, for it suggests that "A *Mist* (or *flood*) probably refers to the water which surged up from the subterranean ocean, the source of fertility."[5] If it did not rain, certainly all circulated water must have issued as springs or rivers from beneath, and this circumstance meant that Eden's Garden, no less than any other part of the earth's surface, was dependent upon the waters of the Deep.

This dependence carried with it the threat as well as the promise of flux. B. W. Anderson, drawing together the biblical views on water for the *Interpreter's Dictionary of the Bible*, chooses to explicate this pronounced ambiguity of the Deep in terms of diverse origins. The normative Hebrew perspective, he suggests, illustrated in such passages as Isaiah 41:17-20 and 43:19-26, sees water as a friendly element even when the source of the water is the primeval Deep (as in Gen. 2:6 49:25; Deut. 33:13; Ezek. 47:1). In another tradition, however, "derived ultimately from the mythological views of Egypt, Mesopotamia, and Canaan, water is regarded as a foe which God overcomes."[6] Anderson stresses, quite properly, the biblical confidence that the threat of flux is not to be taken as any qualification of God's sovereignty, particularly of his freedom in creating the world. The suppressed original myth is perpetrated in Scripture only as marginal poetic metaphors in Job, Isaiah, and the Psalms.[7] A. J. Wensinck in his seminal work, *The Ocean in the Literature of the Western Semites* (1918), also stresses the profound ambiguity of the Deep: "[The] double character of the ocean may be considered indubitable. Tehom is the element of death as well as of life; it is the seat of hell and of paradise."[8] If God's walking and speaking with Adam in the Garden portended a call which would lead beyond the enclave, and structure the whole of man's wayfaring, the reliance even of Eden upon the waters of the Deep indicated the radical openness of world and of way, an openness which vocation would structure but not curtail.

Fidelity to his scriptural model, we can see, does not leave Milton without resources in engaging those powerful influences of his time which combined to breach the historical Eden. His acknowledgment of the Deep figures prominently, as I shall show in Chapter Two, in the implicit theodicy of *Paradise Lost*; the profound ambiguity of the abyssal waters he recognizes, but insists upon their history-long divine regulation and channeling. And his acknowledgment of the divine vocation which leads Adam and Eve beyond Eden is carefully implemented in imagery of finitude rectified and consummated, which he shares with other important figures of the age.

1.2 The Heavenly Life

The conversation between Michael and Adam at the close of *Paradise Lost* has been a special inspiration for recent scholarship on Miltonic versions of paradise more commodious than Eden. Adam declares to Michael, following his education through prophetic vision:

16

> Henceforth I learn, that to obey is best,
> And love with fear the only God, to walk
> As in his presence, ever to observe
> His providence, and on him sole depend.   (XII. 561-4)

To which Michael replies,

> This having learnt, thou has attain'd the sum
> Of wisdom, hope no higher.
>   . . . [O]nly add
> Deeds to thy knowledge answerable, add Faith;
> Add Virtue, Patience, Temperance, add Love.
>   . . . [T]hen wilt thou not be loath
> To leave this Paradise, but shalt possess
> A paradise within thee, happier far.   (XII. 575-587, *passim*)

Louis Martz took the key phrase here, "A paradise within," and used it to title and to shape his study of Augustinian meditation as an influence upon the poetry of the period; but surely Joseph Duncan is right in locating the primary reference of Michael's words simply in the promise of a regenerate, or rectified life and in fact Duncan is able to find any number of discussions contemporary with Milton which adduce such an equivalence between paradise and Christian regeneration.[9] Describing regenerate life, or finitude rectified, the paradise within is to be associated with ideal way rather than ideal haven, and in Milton's work, as in his context, the models invoked were those of pilgrimage, vocation, and "the heavenly life." The last phrase is set off to mark its idiomatic use in the period. I shall be featuring it, for the idea behind it had a significant, if in modern times unnoticed, elaboration in Milton's age, and attending to it properly can illuminate certain perennially puzzling elements of *Paradise Lost*, as well as advance the discussion of paradise.

Milton in his *Christian Doctrine* distinguishes two stages in the glorification of the regenerate man which we may use to provide a basic nomenclature for discussing the heavenly life. Glorification, he says, is the second part (he had earlier discussed communion as the first) "of that growth which is related to Father and Son." Such glorification

is either INCOMPLETE or COMPLETE. INCOMPLETE GLORIFICATION means that WE ARE JUSTIFIED AND ADOPTED BY GOD THE FATHER AND ARE FILLED WITH A CERTAIN AWARENESS BOTH OF PRESENT GRACE AND DIGNITY AND OF FUTURE GLORY, SO THAT WE HAVE ALREADY BEGUN TO BE BLESSED.[10]

It is noteworthy that Milton identified both sorts of glorification with growth in the Christian life, thereby implying that process has its proper place even

17

in the heavenly consummation. And in earthly life the believer is "filled" with a consciousness of the glory to come. This awareness, only modestly described in his discussion of regeneration in *Christian Doctrine*—although Milton's boldness in imaginatively entering Heaven in *Paradise Lost*, Book III encourages us to take it as a fundamental assurance of the poet—we can find to have a voluminous development in Milton's context.

Pervasive in Puritan preaching and writing about Heaven, traceable to the explicit encouragements of John Calvin, was the notion that every Christian might and ought to claim a present access to heaven. The result was that in vision and in "conversation" (i.e., daily conduct) a proleptic marriage of this life and the next was taught. The explicitness and temerity of the claims I think to be well illustrated by Richard Baxter writing in *The Saints Everlasting Rest* (1650).

> Surely the Lord is not now so terrible and inaccessible, nor the passage of Paradise so blocked up, as when the Law and Curse reigned? Wherefore finding, Beloved Christians, that a new and Living way is consecrated for us, through the vail, the flesh of Christ, *by which we may with boldness enter into the Holiest, by the blood of Jesus; I shall draw neer with the fuller Assurance*: and finding the flaming Sword removed, shall look ... into the Paradise of our God: and because I know that this is no forbidden fruit; and withal that it is good for food, and pleasant to the Spiritual Eyes, and a tree to be desired to make one truly wise and happy; I shall take (through the assistance of the Spirit) and eat thereof myself, and give to you (according to my power) that you may eat.[11]

Regeneration and the gift of the Spirit meant for Baxter a present vision of paradise, with a renewed access to the once-forbidden tree of knowledge.

Anticipating Richard Baxter was Joseph Hall (1574-1656), the Puritan-leaning Bishop of Norwich and Exeter, who in a variety of works developed the conviction that a present access to heaven was the prerogative of every Christian. In his little tract, *The Christian*, he offers in twelve succinct sections a description of the title-figure. "His disposition," Hall assures his reader, "hath in it as much of Heaven, as his Earth may make room for." Indeed,

> He walks on Earth, but converses in Heaven; having his Eyes fixed on the invisible, and enjoying a sweet Communion with his God, and Saviour; while all the rest of the World sit in Darkness, he lives in a perpetual Light; the Heaven of Heavens is open to none but him; thither his Eye pierceth, and beholds those Beams of inaccessible Glory which shine in no Face but his.[12]

This remarkable vision, Hall soon declares, carries fixity of mind as its condition. The Christian "will not suffer his Saviour to be ever out of his eye."

Should he lapse, he is "now so much the more fixed by his former slackening, so as he will henceforth sooner part with his soul than his Redeemer." Such fixity of mind Milton, of course, explores in "Il Penseroso," where at the last it carries the promise of heavenly vision like that described by Hall. The "pealing Organ" and "full voic'd Choir," as apprehended by the "fixed mind,"

> may with sweetness, through mine ear,
> Dissolve me into ecstasies,
> And bring all Heav'n before mine eyes.   (164-166)

It is in particular the expansiveness of the claim here ("all Heav'n," no less) which suggests an early link between Milton and the heavenly-mindedness of Puritan tradition.

In the second section of his tract Hall offers a vignette of the Christian stance which in considerable detail anticipates that of Milton the epic poet envisioning the universe.

> The true posture of a Christian then, is this, He sees still Heaven open to him, and beholds and admires the Light inaccessible; He sees the all-glorious God ever before him; The Angels of God about him; The Evil Spirits aloof off enviously grudging, and repining at him; The World under his Feet, willing to rebel, but forced to be subject.... He sees Heaven open with Joy and Desire of Fruition; He sees God with an adoring Awfulness; He sees the Angels with a thankful Acknowledgment, and care not to offend them.... [13]

Surely in such holy courage, which shies not at the divine presence, we have a notable precedent for Milton's visionary ascent in *Paradise Lost*, Book III. Hall continues,

> Having thus gathered up his Thoughts, and found where he is, he may now be fit for his constant devotion; which he falls upon, not without a trembling Veneration of that infinite and incomprehensible Majesty, before whom he is prostrate; now he climbs up into that Heaven, which before he did but behold; and solemnly pours out his Soul, in hearty Thanksgivings, and humble supplications into the Bosom of the Almighty.

Such claims, while at first sight a bit preposterous, were an organic part of that meditation upon the future life which Calvin had enjoined upon every believer. The Reformer's position is artfully summed up for us by Ronald S. Wallace:

> Calvin insists that we can even now in actual practice not only rise with Christ from the death of sin into a new life, but also ascend with Christ above this world.... Indeed, says Calvin, we must ascend now with Christ

if we do not wish to be separated from Him, for He has entered His heavenly life in order that He might "draw believers after him." Calvin can utter a warning against a devotion that stops short with the risen Christ and does not ascend to Heaven with Him to seek happiness there. "Ascension follows resurrection: hence if we are the members of Christ we must ascend into Heaven, because He, in being raised up from the dead was *received up into Heaven* that He might draw us with him."[14]

Wallace goes on to demonstrate how these beliefs were applied by Calvin in the practice of *meditatio futurae vietae* which made possible a disciplined Christian pilgrimage by keeping the heavenly ends ever present to the wayfarer.[15] The crucial point here seems to be the injunction to the believer to implement in the present life the significance of participation in the exalted Christ. To be "in" the heavenly Christ was necessarily to be in Heaven now, whatever the appearances. Richard Sibbes argues the claim in these words: "We must not think of him [the glorified Christ] as an abstracted head severed from us, but think of his glory, and our glory in him and by him."[16] Under the scriptural metaphors of head and body, as well as of bridegroom and spouse, the present glory of the exalted Christ was to be understood as shared with the Church. Sibbes develops both metaphors in his *Excellency of the Gospel*:

> The glory to come is *present to Christ our head*. We, in our husband, are in heaven. Now he hath taken heaven for us! ... To faith, glory to come is present, present in Christ, and we are part of Christ, Christ mystical, and members. And we in our head are in heaven already, and sit there.[17]

In addition to this special understanding of participation in the heavenly Christ, the Calvinist assurance about present access to heaven would seem to rest upon a new understanding of how place was consecrated. We recall that Milton, in disposing of the earthly paradise, asserts that no longer does sanctity attach to place, unless it is brought by those who frequent there. Those definitions of the church which drew upon Calvin tended to emphasize saintly person rather than holy place, and in the writings of Calvinist heavenly-mindedness this distinction quite logically led to an expanded definition of the heavenly.

A meditation by Bishop Hall describes the writer's making his peace with this idea—a commonplace, it would seem, that he could not at first accept.

> I was wont to say, It is in vain for a Man to hope for, and impossible for him to enjoy a double Heaven; one below, and another above: since our sufferings here on Earth must make way for our future Glory: But, now I find it in a better Sense, very feasible for a true Christian to attain both: For, as we say, where the Prince resides, there is the Court; so, surely,

where the supreme and infinite Majesty pleases to manifest his Presence, there is Heaven. . . . [18]

And he concludes with the prayer, "O my God, do thou thus set my Foot over the Threshold of thy Heaven." Given this identification of heaven with the locus of the divine presence, should we wonder that a convention of the time was to identify the Church as an immediate (lower) heaven? Richard Sibbes so speaks of it in his *A Breathing after God* (1639), having earlier cautioned his audience in *Light from Heaven* (1638) that "If heaven be not entred into here, it shall never be entred afterwards."[19] And in his definitive sermon on the matter, *A Glance of Heaven* (1638), Sibbes makes observations about the heaven of the church-service which in their strong evocation of Henry Vaughan suggest that this particular emphasis of Calvinist heavenly-mindedness was by no means restricted to overtly Puritan writing.

> [T]here is nothing in heaven but God's children have a taste of it before they come there in some measure. They have a taste of the communion that is in heaven, in the communion they have on earth: they have a taste of that eternal Sabbath, by some relish they have of holy exercises in these Christian Sabbaths. A Christian is as much in heaven as he can be, when he sanctifies the holy Sabbath, speaking to God in the congregation by prayer, and hearing God speak to him in the preaching of the word.[20]

Vaughan says much the same in describing the joys of the Lord's Day:

> Bright shadows of true Rest! some shoots of blisse,
> Heaven once a week;
> The next worlds gladnes prepossest in this;
> A day to seek
> Eternity in time. . . . [21]

It is, he adds, "Transplanted Paradise," "Heaven here" and "A Taste of Heav'n on earth; the pledge, and cue / Of a full feast." The tags of the tradition are evident.

With such bold assurances tendered by Hall, Sibbes and Baxter for their context, Milton's invocations which open Books I and III of *Paradise Lost* do not, we must conclude, ask for any extraordinary elevation of mind and heart. The humblest Christian, following in the line of the Calvinist exhortations, was so to approach the present heavenly realities. "What in me is dark," Milton had asked in Book I, "Illumine, what is low raise and support; / That to the highth of this great Argument / I may assert Eternal Providence" (22-25). And in Book III, he had prayed, "So much the rather thou Celestial Light / Shine inward . . . that I may see and tell / Of things invisible to mortal sight" (51-52, 55-56). But the enjoyment of such elevation and illumination, at least insofar as heavenly reality was concerned, was the commonplace injunction upon all believers, not merely the epic poet.

Nor should we wonder when Milton moves from the invocation of Book III into an audience with the Trinity unmediated by any angelic narrator or sainted Beatrice. Such audience with the Godhead, such visionary penetration of the innermost precincts of the heavenly, would appear to be an ordinary claim of that heavenly-mindedness which expanded upon Calvin's exhortations to the Christian pilgrim. We can infer, moreover, from Baxter's fearless plucking of the tree of knowledge, that present in Puritan tradition was an understanding of regeneration which made natural the identification with the divine perspective upon good and evil. Truly to know the good, of course, must be to hear the justice of the Father's words about man and his "faithless Progeny," and to grasp the non-patronizing irony of the heavenly laughter that attends the War in Heaven.[22]

The regenerate life enjoying such present access to Heaven, or what Milton calls "incomplete glorification," was at the level of the individual a version of the marriage of earth and heaven already realized. A foreshadowing of the consummation, it presented in history a joining of felicity and process. It was nothing less than a paradisal career, or what Baxter designated the "heavenly life." The continuity between earth and heaven was signally emphasized. Hall writes:

> For, what is Grace here but Glory begun? And what is Glory above but Grace perfected? Whosoever therefore here hath pitch'd the Eye of his faith upon the Invisible, doth but continue His Prospect when he comes to Heaven; the Place is changed, the object is the same, the Act more compleat.[23]

It is, of course, in *Paradise Regained* that Milton provides us his normative example of finitude rectified, though he there speaks less of the presence of heaven than of Eden. Eden, however, must be read as metaphor for heavenly reality. This Edenic beatitude does not follow upon Christ's regeneration, but rather upon the proving of his perfect conformity to divine vocation, and this way of recovering Eden would appear to be exemplary for all men. The opening paragraph of the poem runs

> I who erewhile the happy Garden sung,
> By one man's disobedience lost, now sing
> Recover'd Paradise to all mankind,
> By one man's firm obedience fully tried
> Through all temptation, and the Tempter foil'd
> In all his wiles, defeated and repul'st,
> And *Eden* rais'd in the waste Wilderness.

What is this Eden raised in the wilderness, an Eden raised well before Christ's passion and resurrection which traditionally were thought to seal man's redemption? How, indeed, has the slender action of *Paradise Regained* wrapped *anything* up? The poem's logic plainly assumes an exalted concept of the ultimacy of reconciliation with vocation. In his temptations Jesus confronts basic vocational alternatives, and, in turning them down, he fixes decisively upon a course which means for himself, as it models for the Christian, a rectifying of this finite life. When at the close he stands balanced, it is by virtue of that perfect equanimity, that even-mindedness, which betokens a man wholly conformed to his calling. In this fixity of holy purpose, even in the waste wilderness of this world, may Eden be found.[24]

1.3   Earth's Marriage

A third version of Paradise—that consummated union of earth and heaven which means beatitude not only for individuals but for nature and the entire community of man—was for Milton, as for others in his Age, the highest reach of human aspiration, and the sublimest promise of scripture. Milton addresses the issue in words Raphael speaks to Adam:

> Time may come when men
> With Angels may participate, and find
> No inconvenient Diet, or too light Fare:
> And from these corporal nutriments perhaps
> Your bodies may at last turn all to spirit,
> Improved by tract of time, and wing'd ascend
> Ethereal, as wee, or may at choice
> Here or in Heav'nly Paradises dwell.... (V. 493-500)

These "Heav'nly Paradises" Raphael mentions are not automatically to be preferred to the earth, we notice, and given the embodiedness of Milton's angels we must be cautious in reading "turn all to spirit" as the subliming out of existence of human corporeality. Safest it is, undoubtedly, to understand even "Heav'nly Paradises" as examples of finitude consummated. Such beatitude Milton describes in terms of completed glorification which, he says, "consists in eternal and utterly happy life, arising chiefly from the sight of God." This glorification "will be accompanied by the renovation of, and our possession of, heaven and earth and all those creatures in both which may be useful or delightful to us."[25] Though a believer in the sleep of the soul between death and resurrection, Milton insists that man will rise with the same identity he enjoyed before. "If this were not so we should not be like Christ. He entered into glory with that very same body, that very same flesh

23

and blood, with which he had died and risen again."[26] Here, once again, is the linking of man's glorified state (whether partial or completed) to the significance of the exalted Christ. Milton, we notice, roundly affirms the preservation and transfiguration of earthly particularities implicit in the elevation of the Christ in his "very same flesh and blood."

Now if the career of the paradisal enclave in Milton's century had its paradigmatic case in the depreciation of islands, I suppose the paradigmatic case for earth's marriage was the motif of man's entrance into the celestial spheres. By virtue of the telescope, as Marjorie Nicolson has shown, 17th-century man came to stand among the spheres, and his presence there was nothing less than the breaching of the traditional heaven.[27]

Milton's birth (December 21, 1608) barely antedated Galileo's sighting of spots on the sun in 1609. The latter event signalled an amazingly rapid alteration in the intellectual European's grasp of the skies. In a twinkling, man's gaze contaminated the entirety of the visible cosmos. The stretches of sky beyond the orbit of the moon ceased to be Deep Heaven, and became instead the outer darkness, in the old idiom an apt euphemism for Hell, but in the new idiom a description for a neutral domain which, once the light of science was cast into its corners, would show a comforting conformity to the Periodical Table and the laws of the new physics.

But what Marjorie Nicolson chooses not to develop, though a truth central to our considerations here, is that man's presence among the spheres could be, and was, understood to be the seal of a new liaison no less than it was the dissolution of an old. The breaching of the spheres forced upon the poetic imagination, much as had the decline of sacred geography, a conceiving of the paradisal in which process had a fuller role.

In detailing this development we cannot escape the crucial part played by John Donne. In any number of particulars, his portrayal of how Christ and the glorified (and departed) soul of a Christian believer might join the spheres anticipates Milton's vision of good consummated. I turn then to Donne, expecting to show that events at the opening of Milton's age are of a piece with events at its close.

In "Good Friday, 1613" and the Second Anniversary we have two remarkably prompt responses to the threat posed by Galileo's telescope. The poems date from the same year in Donne's career, at a time when he was struggling with questions of vocation as well as of world-view. For a heaven now admitting the contaminant of man's prideful presence, each poem offers the inevitable medicine: human presence of a sort which heals and mends.

"Good Friday, 1613" offers this consolation in two ways. In an opening conceit, the energy of human devotion is set off against the influence of the prime mover transferred down through the heavenly spheres. It is the first of these energies which Donne honors, and so elevates the significance of man's role in the heavens. Secondly, in a memorable image, the Christ is seen standing imposed on the entire cosmos of nesting spheres. What the God-Man unites and tunes, we gather, no science may fragment.

To develop the first of these arguments, I quote the opening ten lines:

> Let mans Soule be a Spheare, and then, in this,
> The intelligence that moves, devotion is,
> And as the other Spheares, by being growne
> Subject to forraigne motions, lose their owne,
> And being by others hurried every day,
> Scarce in a yeare their naturall forme obey:
> Pleasure or businesse, so, our Soules admit
> For their first mover, and are whirld by it.
> Hence is't, that I am carryed towards the West
> This day, when my Soules forme bends toward the East.[28]

Devotion inclines him to the East, scene of the first Good Friday, but business obliges him to ride westward. Contrived though it may be, the thought seems innocent enough until we grasp the audacity of the full equation: while devotion is the angelic "intelligence" of man's sphere, "pleasure or businesse," *foreign to the soul*, corresponds to the impulse from God the first mover. I suppose most readers are not dismayed by the audacity here; but it should not obscure the claim Donne makes. The centrifugal energy of human devotion, moving out from the human center, is more important to the regime of righteousness in the universe at large than can be those imposed influences Donne identifies with the traditional moving of the spheres. Whether divine grace be understood to prompt human devotion (thereby moving man from within as well as from without) is beside the point. The new prominence of the human figure in the order of the heavens is the plain import of Donne's imagery.

If the opening ten lines magnify the role of human devotion among the spheres, they also prepare for the more memorable image of the cosmic Christ. The poet tells us that, in his imperfect contrition, he is almost glad he is not seeing that weighty spectacle of which the East would remind him.

> Could I behold those hands which span the Poles,
> And tune all spheares at once, peirc'd with those holes?
> Could I behold that endlesse height which is
> Zenith to us, and to'our Antipodes,
> Humbled below us? (21-25a)

This is a vision which the speaker can scarcely give eye to, though he offers his back "to receive / Corrections, till thy mercies bid thee leave." The picture is more than meditative composition to evoke contrition, however. The image directly addresses the same problem Donne is considering in the Second Anniversary: the breaching and mending of the spheres. Significantly, it is the exalted Christ, both God and man, who tunes the spheres. What man may desecrate in a prideful "New Philosophy," man, in the person of Christ, has forever tuned. And in Christ, whose "endlesse height" reaches to the opposed limits of the universe, all of space is forever comprehended. No corner is excluded from that harmonizing rule.

The role which in "Good Friday, 1613" is implicitly ascribed to the exalted Christ, is in the Second Anniversary or "The Progresse of the soul" explicitly ascribed to Elizabeth Drury. The First Anniversary offered an "Anatomy of the World," which in fact amounted to a post mortem on the world's cadaver, and for that dire state of affairs the second poem proposes the curious remedy of the translation to heaven, through the intervening spheres, of a virtuous fifteen-year-old English maid.

> But ere shee can consider how shee went,
> At once is at, and through the Firmament.
> And as these stars were but so many beades
> Strunge on one string, speed undistinguish'd leades
> Her through those spheares, as through the beades, a string,
> Whose quicke succession makes it still one thing:
> As doth the Pith, which, least our Bodies slacke,
> Strings fast the little bones of necke, and backe;
> So by the soule doth death string Heaven and Earth,
> For when our soule enjoyes this her third birth,
> (Creation gave her one, a second, grace,)
> Heaven is as neare, and present to her face,
> As colours are, and objects, in a roome
> Where darknesse was before, when Tapers come.[29]   (205-216)

Conspicuous here is the insistence that Elizabeth Drury, "our Soule," unites Heaven and Earth, and the double meaning of "our Soule" is not to be overlooked. The immediacy of heaven, moreover, is associated with what is ever present, but visible only when light is introduced.

Her swift passage to heaven is at once a binding and a humanizing of the spheres. That virtuous presence—the withdrawal of which from our earth, the First Anniversary had assured us, meant its lifelessness and decay—is in this poem nothing less than the new *anima mundi*, animating the entire sequence of spheres, not merely earth. It was the *idea* of the girl not Miss Drury herself which the poem set out to celebrate—or so Ben Jonson reported Donne's defense of his argument—but I find a further broadening of the reference to be suggested by the problem we know the poem is addressing. The translation of *any* virtuous Christian soul must have the same effect: the heavenly order is altered. The sidereal is now to be apprehended, not merely in terms of a secular and profaning attention, but also in terms of a regenerate human presence which weds human particularity and process to the spheres.

Such transfigured particularity Donne had represented in "Good Friday, 1613" in the scars of the hands spanning the poles. Here it is the "accidental" (i.e., non-essential) joys which Elizabeth Drury, the type for all redeemed persons, introduces as new and lasting features into the heavenly landscape. The man who does not strive the more for heaven knowing Elizabeth Drury is there, says Donne,

> he doth not know
> That accidentall joyes in Heaven doe grow.   (381-382)

Only in Heaven, the poet goes on,

> joies strength is never spent;
> And accidentall things are permanent.   (487-488)

He then brilliantly claims for the consummate reality that same sort of mutability, or process not admitting of decay or decline, which Spenser had claimed in the Mutabilitie Cantos, and which Donne had facetiously claimed for his profane love in "Loves Growth." Here, of a certainty, is process idealized:

> Joy of a soules arrivall neere decaies;
> For that soule ever joyes, and ever staies.
> Joy that their last great Consummation
> Approaches in the resurrection;
> When earthly bodies more celestiall
> Shalbe, then Angels were, for they could fall;
> This kind of joy doth every day admit
> Degrees of grouth, but none of loosing it.   (489-96)

This heavenly perfection is ever changing, ever fixed. Elizabeth Drury

> by making full perfection grow,
> Peeces a Circle, and still keepes it so,
> Long'd for, and longing for'it, to heaven is gone,
> Where shee receives, and gives addition.   (507-510)

This new covenant, joining earthly things and heavenly, is the "Proclamation" which Elizabeth Drury epitomizes at the close, and for which Donne presents himself as summoning "Trumpet." The claim is extravagant; or is it? The deftness with which Donne recasts the significance of man's breaching of the spheres is remarkable. What was mortal threat, a perforation of the heavenly spaces which promised a wholesale profanation of the superlunary, he is able to present, in the figure of Elizabeth Drury's virtuous and regenerate soul, as the human joining of orders. Appropriately, he marshalls arguments for growth, enhancement, dilation in heaven which serve to highlight the role of time, or earthly process in the heavenly order. And in stressing the place of the "accidental joy" in heaven, in marking out the role of one particular soul in changing the contents of heaven, he carries out the implications of the presence of the exalted and human Christ in heaven which Calvin and Calvinist heavenly-mindedness had also glimpsed.

Recalling Milton's insouciance about committing himself to a Ptolemaic or Copernican astronomy in *Paradise Lost*, we ought not to be surprised that the Donneian image of man's breaching the spheres is nowhere to be found in Milton, although we have seen how the narrative framework of Book III logically entails such a penetration by Milton the regenerate seer. It seems likely, moreover, that Milton's readiness to detail the accidentals of activity in heaven—e.g., the paraphernalia of rebellion and war—is the correlate of his thorough-going introduction of a human perspective in the heavenly places.

But Milton's relating of earth's marriage to the imagery of the spheres is most explicit in several provocative figures suggesting how movement is perfected in the heavenly consummation. One of these, the "orb of joy," occurs in his *The Reason of Church Government* (1642). The passage I cite has been oft-quoted, C. S. Lewis, for example, referring to it in order to demonstrate Milton's strong approbation of religious obedience.[30] I believe its primary significance to lie in its artful encapsulation of Milton's understanding of ideal process. Explaining to his reader that a disciplined life is not necessarily tedious, Milton turns to the glorified lives of the saints in heaven.

> Yet is it not to be conceived that those eternal effluences of sanctity and love in the glorified saints should by this means be confined and cloyed with repetition of that which is prescribed, but that our happiness may orb itself into a thousand vagancies of glory and delight, and with a kind of eccentrical equation be, as it were, an invariable planet of joy and felicity.[31]

The "vagancies" of the soul are, in fact, wanderings; but the totality of the soul's movement is orderly since the divine ordination perfectly reconciles Christian liberty with that disciplined response to calling which Milton is prescribing for the Church.

I think it accurate to say that throughout Milton's age the perfection of movement is represented by such analogies between the human career and the orbits of the heavenly bodies. Though the equating of obedient career with orbicular movement was ancient, the seventeenth century witnesses a new willingness to stress by means of such imagery not the disjunction of earth and heaven, but their promised union.

For Milton the orb of joy, understood by analogy with the angel-informed spheres of the medieval astronomy to be the inclusive locus of obedient action, was inevitably cast also as globe of light. In the Nativity Ode the radiant globe was a phalanx of angels organized for praise, and in *Paradise Regained* Christ is carried to a bower of restorative rest by a "fiery globe" of ministering angels; the formation is a common one in *Paradise Lost*. The diffusion of its reference to cover circumstances of redemptive "heavenly" work by man in history should not surprise us. This is certainly what we have in a memorable description of the Long Parliament in Milton's *An Apology for Smectymnuus*. This Parliament was formed, says Milton,

> God and man consenting in joint approbation to choose them out as worthiest above others to be both the great reformers of the church, and the restorers of the commonwealth. Nor did they deceive that expectation which with the eyes and desires of their country was fixed upon them: for no sooner did the force of so much united excellence meet in one globe of brightness and efficacy, but encountering the dazzled resistance of tyranny, they gave not over, though their enemies were strong and subtle, till they had laid her grovelling upon the fatal block; with one stroke winning again our lost liberties and charters, which our forefathers after so many battles could scarce maintain.[32]

The closing image suggests that summary stroke of justice from the "two-handed engine" of *Lycidas*, but the more significant image is the "one globe of brightness and efficacy." To speak thus of the Long Parliament is to identify it with both the perfect obedience of the celestial spheres, and the redemptive activity of the angelic phalanx.[33]

Milton's words (in *Christian Doctrine*) about the necessary incompleteness of glorification in this life should caution us, however, against taking his figurative description of the Long Parliament as anything more than a foreshadowing of that wholly glorified activity which will characterize the marriage of earthly and heavenly. On the matter of the perfection of action in consummate reality, Milton's sympathies seem more akin to those of Richard Baxter than to those of Joseph Hall, however much the three writers share by way of confidence about the continuity of this life and the next. Milton, like Baxter, portrays for us a beatitude in which the ancient opposition of activity and perfection is not finally honored. Ultimate perfection

29

need not be total freedom from movement. Joseph Hall, on the other hand, is not so careful to divorce perfection from motionlessness.

Milton's position on the matter we can find abundantly displayed in his deployment of angels throughout the universe of *Paradise Lost* and *Paradise Regained*. It is the métier of his angels to be active, and they are by no means bound to the Ptolemaic spheres. Adam assures Eve, as they move to "thir blissful Bower," that God will never want for praise, even when they are sleeping:

> Millions of spiritual Creatures walk the Earth
> Unseen, both when we wake, and when we sleep:
> All these with ceaseless praise his works behold
> Both day and night.   (*PL*, IV. 677-680)

This angelic activity, which we must infer pervades the entire created order, as well as heaven, is praise, but it is also "walk." The angels "keep watch" and make music "With Heav'nly touch of instrumental sounds." And no one who has read Milton's two epics can doubt that his angels enjoy both mobility and versatility. Their actions would seem to bear the promise of what Milton describes in *Christian Doctrine*, under the rubric of "complete glorification," as the possession of heaven and earth, and "all those creatures in both which may be useful or delightful to us."[34]

Richard Baxter, similarly, in *The Saint's Everlasting Rest* assures his reader that he must not misconstrue the saint's "Rest" as inertness. No,

> This Rest containeth A Sweet and constant Action of all the Powers of the Soul and Body in this fruition of God. It is not the Rest of a stone, which ceaseth from all motion, when it attains the Center.

The glorified body will forever sound forth praises of God.

> And if the Body shall be thus employed, Oh how shall the Soul be taken up? As its powers and capacities are greatest, so its actions strongest, and its enjoyment sweetest. As the bodily senses have their proper aptitude and action, whereby they receive and enjoy their objects: so doth the Soul in its own action enjoy its own object: By knowing, by thinking and Remembering, by Loving, and by delightful joying.[35]

Baxter is particularly vivid in describing the activity of memory, which we recognize as that faculty most important to the effectual marriage of earth and heaven for the individual soul:

> [T]he Memory will not be Idle, or useless, in this Blessed work. If it be but by looking back, to help the soul to value its enjoyment, Our knowledg will be enlarged, not diminished; therefore the knowledge of things past shall not be taken away. And what is that knowledg, but Remembrance?

Doubtless from that height, the Saint can look behind him and before him. ... To stand on that Mount, whence we can see the Wilderness and Canaan both at once, to stand in Heaven, and look back on earth, and weigh them together in the ballance of a comparing sense and judgment, how must it needs transport the soul. (*SER*, p. 33)

Surely it is significant that this perfection of integrated activity, mobilizing all the faculties of the soul, is associated by Baxter not only with the glorified life but with heavenly meditation here. In the concert of the soul's faculties in meditation upon heaven, the heavenly consummation is both prefigured and tasted.

This meditation is the acting of all the powers of the soul. Its the work of the Living, and not of the dead. Its a work of all others most spiritual and sublime, and therefore not to be well performed by a heart that's merely carnal and terrene. Also they must necessarily have some relation to heaven, before they can familiarly there converse. (*SER*, p. 690)

Such an exact anticipation of heavenly activity in meditation must mean a present heavenly joy. Throughout *The Saint's Everlasting Rest*, Baxter has insisted that to be heavenly-minded is to be joyous, in heaven now. "A heavenly minde is a joyful minde: This is the nearest and the truest way to live a life of comfort," he declares (*SER*, p. 606). "When is it that you have largest comforts? Is it not after such an exercise as this, when thou hast got up thy heart, and converst with God, and talkt with the inhabitants of the higher world, and viewed the mansions of the Saints and Angels, and filled thy soul with the forethoughts of Glory?" (*SER*, p. 607). This confidence, which we see so fully exploited by Milton in *Paradise Lost*, Baxter sums up in his later work *The Life of Faith* (1660): the life of faith "consisteth in the *daily sight of heaven*."[36]

Is it not such a foretaste of the perfection of heavenly activity which Henry Vaughan so often describes with the imagery of calm? So, in "The Constellation":

> Fair, order'd lights (whose motion without noise
> Resembles those true Joys
> Whose spring is on that hil where you do grow
> And we here tast sometimes below,)
> With what exact obedience do you move....[37]

And again, in "Mount of Olives":

> When first I saw true beauty, and thy Joys
> Active as light, and calm without all noise
> Shin'd on my soul, I felt through all my powr's

31

> Such a rich air of sweets, as Evening showrs
> Fand by a gentle gale Convey.... [38]

The Mount of Olives, by virtue of having provided a retreat for Christ in his earthly sojourn, as well as the site of his ascension, and the presumed site of his return, was for meditative writers like St. Ignatius Loyola and St. Francois de Sales, and conspicuously for Vaughan (who has a prose meditative tract as well as two poems using the motif for title) the locus for a meditative joining of earth and heaven. The utter tranquillity, yet activity, of these anticipatory joys reflect that oxymoronic combination of motion and rest which had long been associated with the spheres.

I suggested above that although Milton, like Baxter, insists upon a perfection of movement as sign of the consummate state of affairs, Bishop Hall is not so careful to preserve the paradox. I was referring to the final meditation in Hall's *Soliloquies*, where he would seem to suggest that while the heaven of the spheres (the lower heaven in his scheme) is indeed one of perfected motion, the soul will leave such behind when it moves to the Empyrean to be with God.

> And as thou, O my God, has a double Heaven, a lower Heaven for Motion, and an empyreal Heaven for Rest; one patent to the Eye, the other visible to our Faith; so let my Soul take part with them both; let it ever be moving towards thee, and in thee, (like this visible Heaven) and (since the End of all Motion is Rest) let it ever rest with thee, in that invisible Region of Glory So let it move ever to thee whilst I am here, that it may ever rest with thee in thine eternal Glory hereafter. [39]

Even should we concede some ambiguity in this passage, especially in the phrase "moving ... in thee," it would seem that Hall chooses not to go so far as Donne, Baxter, or Milton, in the range or explicitness of his claims for the preservation of movement in the promised marriage of earth and heaven.

In such consummated finitude, Donne sees a perpetual dilation of the good, the preservation of "accidental joys," and the (implied) decisive contribution of each regenerate soul to the eternal order; Baxter sees a role for every human faculty, including memory (heavenly work in fact being a contiuum with heavenly meditation here); and Milton sees an ample scope for heavenly vocation, the work of men and of angels, articulated as orb of joy, or globe of light. It is tempting to take the famous close of his Sonnet XIX as a wisdom of truly cosmic dimension:

> Thousands at his bidding speed
> And post o'er Land and Ocean without rest:
> They also serve who only stand and wait.

The standing and waiting here I cannot, as some readers of the poem do, take to be Milton's covert elevation of motionlessness above motion, for the final word must mean not only patient service, but also the tarrying for further calling, since for Milton calling like glorification is a normative element in both rectified and consummated finitude.

The final state of affairs, Raphael had disclosed in *Paradise Lost* (VII. 161), is to be "One Kingdom, Joy and Union without end." This must be a Kingdom, we can conclude, which forever joins finite and infinite, rather than scuttling the temporal; it must be a joy which weds what Donne refers to as the "accidental" and the "essential"; it must be a Union which transfigures earthly life even as it preserves it. We have seen how the several primary writers in the reformed tradition of heavenly-mindedness provided supportive context for Milton's asseveration of such continuities, and how man's breaching of the spheres was not merely a contamination of the heavens. With Donne, Baxter, and Milton, the image of man superimposed upon the heavens could be, and was, resolutely interpreted as blessing, through the very simple strategy of deepening the age's understanding of the ancient beliefs about the exaltation of the incarnated Christ, and of resurrection. The presence of regenerate man among the spheres did not need to be construed as threat, but could be grasped as an occasion for exploring the ways in which process was ingredient in the ideal.

CHAPTER TWO
Paradise and Miltonic Theodicy

2.1 Moral and Aesthetic Theodicies

Man's glorification, begun in earthly regenerate life and perpetuated in the union of earth and heaven, does not represent the only rapprochement between process and the ideal given important elaboration in the Age of Milton. The cosmic meliorism which Milton describes in his major poems constitutes another such link. The process of God's history-long curtailment of evil as it conditions human choice and growth, Milton's meliorism is in fact a secondary theodicy ancillary to the more orthodox and public one argued in *Paradise Lost*.

Though both the primary and secondary theodicies in Milton offer to justify God's ways to man, the two schemes do not feature the same paradigm-questions. The primary theodicy asks "Where and how did evil arise in the beginning?" while the secondary theodicy asks "How is God overcoming evil and restoring paradise?" I shall sketch out the shape of each of these schemes before exploring Milton's cosmic meliorism.

Milton's answer to the first question provides, of course, the manifest outlines of story in *Paradise Lost*. God is vindicated by the tracing of all evil back to primordial free creaturely choices: Lucifer's in Heaven, and Adam's and Eve's in the Garden of Eden. This theodicy, which I designate the moral one, is marked by its final authoritativeness for Milton, its preservation of a divinity free from evil or constraint, and its unyielding abstractness. For Christian orthodoxy to this day, it is the final defense of God, although the unconditioned free choice on which all hinges is necessarily beyond coherent representation by art. Absolute freedom is opaque to any observer, whom it must impress as either determined by antecedents, or inexplicable. Hence the abstractness of this argument, whatever the stories it may press into service.

Insisting that God is simply good, as the etymology of his English name implies, the moral theodicy resolutely affirms as well the good of the original creation. The refrain which follows the several creative acts in Genesis 1 is "And God saw that it was good." The final refrain runs, "And God saw everything that he had made, and behold, it was very good." Here is the legitimate satisfaction of an artisan who has achieved precisely what he set out to achieve. Nothing has slipped off-center or gone awry.

Whence, then, the manifold impositions upon our health, strength and good temper which the world as we know it so strenuously foists upon us? These all must be traced back to events quite independent of creation. A capsule summary of this position appears in *Paradise Lost*, Book III, in God's exposition to his angels of the future of man.

> So will fall
> Hee and his faithless Progeny: whose fault?
> Whose but his own?   ingrate, he had of mee
> All he could have; I made him just and right,
> Sufficient to have stood, though free to fall.
> Such I created all th'Ethereal Powers
> And Spirits, both them who stood and them who fail'd;
> Freely they stood who stood, and fell who fell.   (III. 95-102)

The logic here is unimpeachable. For the goodness of God to be preserved, the primordial choice of evil must be understood as utterly free, since if there were conditions on that action, they, or their source, must bear the burden of responsibility.

No close reader of *Paradise Lost*, however, is likely to have missed the difficulties Milton confronted in presenting the crucial free choices in his poem. Here, for example, is Lucifer's choice in heaven:

> he of the first,
> If not the first Arch-Angel, great in Power,
> In favor and preeminence, yet fraught
> With envy against the Son of God, that day
> Honor'd by his great Father, and proclaim'd
> Messiah King anointed, could not bear
> Through pride that sight, and thought himself impair'd.
> Deep malice thence conceiving and disdain,
> Soon as midnight brought on the dusky hour
> Friendliest to sleep and silence, he resolv'd
> With all his Legions to dislodge and leave
> Unworshipt, unobey'd the Throne supreme.... (V. 659-670)

The event that preceded Lucifer's rebellion was, we recall, the Father's elevation of the Son with the imperative that all are to give him special honor. This act, which has the distinction of being the very first happening in the poem (if we stretch Milton's Eternity upon the rack of simple chronology), is in Lucifer's eyes the *casus belli*. Milton, drawing upon diffuse hints from Psalms, Isaiah and Revelation, has provided the necessary point of departure for his narrative, dropping a stone into the untroubled waters of Eternity. But why do the particular effects follow which the passage quoted above describes?

Lucifer is offended. Apparently that transparent embodiment of the general will, which Milton in *Tenure of Kings and Magistrates* insisted was requisite in all lordly decrees, does not obtain here. Lucifer does not see, we must assume, how his own good is effectuated in the new regime. He "thought himself impair'd." If he shows a strange obtuseness in grasping his personal good in the new decree, how much greater is that ignorance of ends which he reveals in his ensuing rebellion. He seems unaware of what separation from God must be, what pain will be, what spiritual death amounts to. In short, he has chosen; but of *what* he has chosen he shows only a fragmentary grasp.

This observation was not without its proponents among Milton's contemporaries. Early in the 17th century, John Salkeld had asserted unequivocally that the rebel angels did not enjoy a vision of God's essence as other angels did.

> [I]f they [the rebels] had once seene cleerely the divine essence, they could not afterward have sinned . . . ; also if they had beene once blessed, they could not have desired any thing more.[2]

While he does not draw out the implications for theodicy, it is evident that such claims must reflect upon the plausibility of the traditional moral defense of God. Indeed, Thomas Traherne calls into question, in his second century of meditations, whether any creature will freely choose its own injury.

> No man can sin that clearly seeth the Beauty of Gods face: Becaus no Man can sin against his own Happiness. that is, none can when he sees it clearly willingly and Wittingly foresake it. Tempter, Temptation, Loss and Danger being all seen.[3]

Yet is it not plain, as we turn from Milton's Lucifer to his Adam and Eve, that the latter cannot, any more than Lucifer, be supposed to know precisely what they choose when they elect to disobey? To press no further the case for ignorance as a circumstance necessary to their lapse, consider their uncertainty about death. In an early exchange with Eve, Adam instructs her about the forbidden tree: they are not to taste

> that only Tree
> Of Knowledge, planted by the Tree of Life,
> So near grows Death to Life, whate'er Death is,
> Some dreadful thing no doubt.   (IV. 423-426)

Though Adam calls Death some "dreadful thing," we must wonder what meaning "dread" can possibly have for either him or his mate in the untroubled felicity of Eden.

The unqualified freedom of Adam's and Eve's choosing of evil is further undermined by the role of Lucifer. Milton pointedly distinguishes between fallen angel on the one hand and fallen man on the other, insisting that the latter is forgiveable while the former is not; the basis for his distinction is the fact of man's temptation.

> Man falls deceiv'd
> By th'other first: Man therefore shall find grace,
> The other none. (III. 131-133)

Milton regards the very experience of temptation from without as extenuating. It is, in other words, a condition upon freedom which must transfer to yet remoter agency the full responsibility for evil. Since only the wholly unconditioned choice has genuine explanatory value in the moral theodicy, the plausibility of that theodicy must suffer from such authorial concessions.

Even so, in thus calling attention to the difficulties hedging about Milton's moral theodicy, I do not wish to dispute it. The ascendancy of diverse deterministic ideologies in our time points up the difficulty, if not the impossibility, of presenting any free choice so that it must appear free to another. Milton's insoluble problems in presenting the free act are of a piece with his problems in presenting the other virtues of paradise. We, for whom good and evil are twins always cleaving together, cannot see any good unqualified by its paired contrary.

To ask about the divine engagement with evil in the immediate moment is, however, to point attention to more submerged elements in Milton's story, elements which in fact articulate what I shall call the implicit aesthetic theodicy.

Aesthetic theodicy keeps in focus the conditions upon creative and moral activity. In the background, of course, is the pagan cosmogony, in which the divine action in creation was compromised by the refractory raw material. Both in the original event, and in the continuing activity of the demiurge, or whatever creative agent is completing creation, the material does not perfectly express the divine intent. This scheme has no need for a myth of the fall to explain the presence of evil in the world. Practically speaking, creation and fall are identified. It is appropriate to call the theodicy associated with this cosmogony the aesthetic one, for two reasons. First, such constraints imposed by the medium or material are immediately recognizable to any artist or craftsman; second, while it does not preserve the unconditioned freedom, and hence goodness of God, this theodicy can argue that the aesthetic considerations of greater richness, intricacy, novelty, in fact legitimate the risks of creation and apparently were attractive enough to impel God to submit himself to the rules governing creative work in the first place.

The aesthetic theodicy—implicit in the narrative if not the expository asides of *Paradise Lost* and *Paradise Regained*, and to some degree in the Nativity Ode and *Samson Agonistes*—focuses not on the free creaturely choice, but rather on the conditioned choice. In the stead of abstract moral evil, this theodicy attends to the substantive evil of those conditions which precipitate and shape creative work (which, in its fullest perfection, will finally transform the evil into greater good). This theodicy we should describe as concrete, practical, and heuristic. Unlike the moral theodicy, it is not etiological, since it offers no clear causal link between God the absolute agent and the conditions affecting his creatures. In this sense, too, it is not ultimate. Its particular relevance as an explanatory model in the present context is its framing the cosmic meliorism Milton is at such pains to develop. Man's choosing and making may be cruelly conditioned, but the conditions are undergoing a perpetual and positive transformation.

I have spoken a bit vaguely about the "conditions" on human choice but Milton supplies clear illustrations of the subject in *Areopagitica* and in *Samson Agonistes* and it is important to have the subject free of confusion before we take up Milton's meliorism. In *Areopagitica* Milton says

> Good and evil we know in the field of this world grow up together almost inseparably; and the knowledge of good is so involved and inter-woven with the knowledge of evil, and in so many cunning resemblances hardly to be discerned, that those confused seeds which were imposed on Psyche as an incessant labor to cull out and sort asunder, were not more intermixed.[4]

While the allusion to the judgment on Psyche is the conspicuous one, the more illuminating one is certainly that at the opening. Good and evil, growing inseparably in the "field of this world" point to two of Jesus' parables which comment upon the conditioning of human choices. The first (Matthew 13: 24-30) tells of good seed sown in a field, only to be contaminated by an enemy's sowing weeds; the resulting crop is so confused, that only at harvest (Judgment Day) can they be expected to be separated. The second (Matthew 13:1-9) is the more familiar story of the sower whose seed falls on various soils, and so comes to varying ends. That seed, in particular, which fell among the thorns had its growth choked by them. In both these stories it is impossible to miss Jesus' own acknowledgment—however vexatious the implications—that human choosing is variously influenced by conditions not of the chooser's making.

For an example of how such conditions are at the heart of the tragic vision, we may turn to the last moments in the career of Milton's Samson. Rousing himself finally to the implications of his freedom, Samson permits himself to be taken to the festival of Dagon. While his hair has grown back, presumably neither his captors, nor he himself until the penultimate moment, realize that heroic acts are once more within his scope. But Samson lives his freedom by going to the pagan temple.

> Commands are no constraints. If I obey them,
> I do it freely. . . . (1372-1373)

In pulling the temple on his own head, however, he suffers conditions not of his choosing. The Chorus plays out this insight:

> Living or dying thou hast fulfill'd
> The work for which thou wast foretold
> To *Israel*, and now li'st victorious
> Among thy slain self-kill'd
> Not willingly, but tangl'd in the fold
> Of dire necessity, whose law in death conjoin'd
> Thee with thy slaughter'd foes in number more
> Than all thy life had slain before. (1661-1668)

God in *Paradise Lost* assures his listeners that he is approached by neither necessity or chance. The same is patently not true for his creatures.

2.2   Milton's Cosmic Meliorism

The implicit aesthetic theodicy of Milton's major poems reveals itself in two principal affirmations:

1. The Chaos which provides a ubiquitous context for the actions of *Paradise Lost* and which Milton closely associates with Lucifer, depicts the radical ambiguity of the conditions influencing creative and moral activity.

2. These chaotic conditions upon human effort are, however, suffering a progressive alteration by the hand of God. The process, indeed, has been marked by at least seven *chairoi*, or dramatic crises, when the scope of Satan and/or Chaos was at a stroke significantly curtailed.

Something like a Fifty Years' War has characterized scholarly discussion of the role Milton's chaos has to play in his cosmogony, following Denis Saurat's suggestion in 1928 that when God says "I uncircumscrib'd myself retire" (VII. 170) he is voicing the Cabbalistic notion of a divine retraction from part of his substance in order to create matter. Saurat's position has been felt by most to lean too far in the direction of dualism. And A. S. P. Woodhouse and A. B. Chambers, Jr., have for now established that Milton is reasonably orthodox in his doctrine of creation even though he does insist that God must be understood as creating out of himself (*ex deo*) rather than out of nothing at all (*ex nihilo*).[5]

Yet the enthusiasm to defend a Miltonic position which respects the unqualified divine omnipotence has a hurdle to clear in Milton's apparent carelessness about suggesting in *Paradise Lost* that God's creative energies may have, indeed, been compromised by his materials. Here is the poet's first description of chaos, which finds Satan peering

> Into this wild Abyss,
> The Womb of nature and perhaps her Grave,
> Of neither Sea, nor Shore, nor Air, nor Fire,
> But all these in thir pregnant causes mixt
> Confus'dly, and which thus must ever fight,
> Unless th'Almighty Maker them ordain
> His dark materials to create more Worlds.... (II. 910-916)

Why "dark materials," one must ask. Were they just as recalcitrant in the first creation? That primary creation had been described in these words:

> but on the wat'ry calm
> His brooding wings the spirit of God outspread,
> And vital virtue infus'd, and vital warmth
> Throughout the fluid Mass, but downward purg'd
> The black tartareous cold Infernal dregs
> Adverse to life.... (VII. 234-239)

We are assured here that the creation involves a precipitation of the "Infernal dregs," but there is no assurance that they are altogether removed from the orbit of human kind. It is one thing to point out, as R. M. Adams has done, that Milton's chaos is a notable pressure upon all the fallen history of man disclosed to Adam by Michael in the closing books of the poem.[6] Such impingement we expect to be part of our fallen lot. But it is quite another thing to intimate, as Milton seems to, that God's "dark materials" in some fashion compromised the original free creation.

Yet, as a contributing detail in that proximate, aesthetic theodicy which Milton presents, this intimation is altogether plausible. For aesthetic theodicy stresses, as I noticed above, the artist's struggle with his materials, with the conditions; that is surely the presiding effect in these cases. In the biblical matrix, the refractoriness of such materials is hinted in the insistent poetic equations among the terms sea, sea monster (Leviathan), hell, and abyss.[7] With this for precedent, it is not surprising to find Milton presenting Lucifer's breaching of Eden in the way that he does.

Lucifer makes two entrances into the Garden in the course of *Paradise*

Lost. Each entrance has its special significance as a kind of transgression. His first suggests the housebreaker:

> One Gate there only was, and that look'd East
> On th'other side: which when th'arch-felon saw
> Due entrance he disdain'd, and in contempt,
> At one slight bound high overleap'd all bound
> Of Hill or highest Wall, and sheer within
> Lights on his feet.   (IV. 178-183)

In his second entrance, made in Book IX, Lucifer is closely associated with the primary ancient image of flux in the garden, that is, with the fountain at its center.

>   There was a place,
> Now not, though Sin, not Time, first wrought the change,
> Where *Tigris* at the foot of Paradise
> Into a Gulf shot under ground, till part
> Rose up a Fountain by the Tree of Life;
> In with the River sunk, and with it rose
> Satan involv'd in rising Mist, then sought
> Where to lie hid. . . .   (IX. 69-76)

No sooner has he entered with the mist or "flood" of the Deep's waters, than he searches for a suitable further vehicle in the Garden.

>   [T]hrough each Thicket Dank or Dry,
> Like a black mist low creeping, he held on
> His midnight search, where soonest he might find
> The Serpent. . . .   (IX. 179-182)

The identification with mist is sustained here, and both mist and Lucifer "low creeping" are associated with the snake soon to be possessed.

Beyond this richly suggestive narrative linking of Lucifer the transgressor with the fountain or mist,[8] we have Lucifer's affinity with chaos as it is suggested in Books II and X. When Lucifer is first cast from Heaven, he plummets through chaos for nine days, unable to check his fall. But soon thereafter the universe is created as God's response to the decimation of his heavenly ranks, and it appears that chaos bears Milton's God a lasting grudge for this encroachment upon his rule. When Lucifer leaves Hell to find the New World, he is given directions by Chaos personified as anarch, and he now proves able to loft himself in the chaotic medium. When later his mission proves successful, Chaos is willing to support a "broad and beat'n way / Over the dark Abyss."

Though Lucifer throughout the poem enjoys, as the remnants of his own

41

creation, the "virtues" of an organized selfhood, and to that extent stands in contrast to the absolute disorder of chaos, he is shown to us as increasingly the instrument of that absolute disorder. We should not wonder at the equivalence which Milton establishes in describing Lucifer after he has received aid from chaos:

> Satan stay'd not to reply,
> But glad that now his Sea should find a shore, ...
> Springs upward like a Pyramid of fire
> Into the wild expanse.   (II. 1010-1011, 1013-1014)[9]

Chaos had earlier been presented as a "dark / Illimitable Ocean," and the import of Milton's designation of Lucifer as "Sea" finding a limit only in the vulnerable shores of the New World is to identify the two arch threats to God's creation.

In collaboration with the Deep, Lucifer is explicitly identified with those conditions which compromise Eve's and Adam's choice and hence make their disobedience forgiveable. I have already cited the lines (III. 131-133) in which Milton's God declares man worthy of grace because of Satan's role as tempter in Eden; it remains to develop something of the background for Satan's penetration of Eden, for on inspection the cumulative effect of the incidents which lead to his appearance there is to suggest the impossibility of imagining the process of human growth and choice apart from the impingement of conditions.

Eden's Garden on the newly created earth is, in the military idiom which *Paradise Lost* so pervasively employs, a strategic outpost of the divine rule. Yet, as strategic outpost, Eden is involved in an extraordinary network of apparent as opposed to real defenses. To read Books III, IV, and IX of *Paradise Lost* is to be impressed with how exposed Eden is to the machinations of evil. While God makes the sundry gestures of posting guard, and of preparing Adam and Eve for Satan's appearance, no guard or sentry proves adequate and, as we remember too well, on the fatal morning Eve meets Satan at the tree without benefit of any resource she did not bring with her.

But the signal disclosure of the vulnerability of Eden comes in the early encounter of Lucifer with Uriel, Regent of the sun,

> one of the sev'n
> Who in God's presence, nearest to his Throne
> Stand ready at command, and are his Eyes
> That run through all the Heav'ns, or down to th'Earth.

> (III. 648-651)

Some lines after this we are assured that indeed Uriel is held to be "The sharpest-sighted Spirit of all in Heav'n" (III. 691). Yet Satan, disguised as a brightly-colored "stripling Cherub," is not recognized by even this keenest eyed of all God's host, since neither angel nor man, the narrator carefully tells us, can see through "Hypocrisy, the only evil that walks / Invisible" (III. 683-684).

Such foreshadowing is remarkably dire. If Uriel, the paragon of vision, is deceived in the first test of Satan's ability to dissemble, there can be little hope for Eve and for Adam. Yet it is not so much the vulnerability of Eden to Satan that I want to notice as it is a subtler point about the conditions upon human choice. Even prelapsarian man, Milton affirms, was vulnerable to the discrepancy between appearance and reality. Such discrepancy, which must needs exonerate any choice made with good heart but defective eye, is alike the bane of angel and man. Milton's concession, taken by itself, must undermine the plausibility of the entire explicit theodicy, which requires, as we have seen, the presumption of absolute creaturely freedom for God to be cleared of complicity.

We have, however, already acknowledged the impossibility of any artist's succeeding in what Milton attempts here, and it is perhaps more useful to notice what Milton's statement concerning hypocrisy says about the process of human growth. If in its extreme and perverse forms the discrepancy between the apparent and the real is to be condemned as affectation and deceit, in its less extreme forms, this discrepancy is indispensable to creaturely change and growth. The process of socialization or, in Yeats' phrase, the pursuit of "active virtue," assumes the mask. One becomes what he pretends to be. The repeated concession becomes the impulse of the heart. So we have all learned to be social, if not virtuous creatures. This "condition" which regulates or constrains the process of growth is, we gather, given its archetypal expression in Lucifer's representation of himself to Uriel, though he sums up the vicious rather than the virtuous accommodation of the fact.

Uriel's inability to recognize Lucifer for what he was encapsulates an intuition which many readers of *Paradise Lost* IV (the description of Eden) must have entertained. Finitude manqué, the paradisal enclave, does not truly make room for growth. To speak of growth, we are obliged to think in aesthetic categories, in terms of raw material being transformed, of conditions overcome, of artifice (appearance) structuring reality. Just as there is no art without stuff, there is no process without scope or amplitude for that process to expand into. This we must grant even if such amplitude (depth, openness, the abysall) inevitably becomes imaged as both promise and threat, thereby obscuring the divine goodness.

Understanding that Lucifer and the Deep express virtually inescapable elements of the ancient mythic speculations about human choosing, we are prepared to turn to the second of Milton's primary affirmations organic to his aesthetic theodicy: the conditions upon creative and moral effort are in fact suffering a progressive amelioration, characterized by *chairoi* of momentous consequences.

Seven such crucial events may be identified in Milton's cosmic history, though others may be hinted in *Paradise Lost* XI-XII.[10] I shall annotate them all briefly, and then spend a bit more time with the one featured in *Paradise Regained*.

The first of these crucial events is also the first of the two climaxes of *Paradise Lost*: the defeat of Lucifer in Heaven, and his banishment to Hell (the second climax is, of course, Adam's fall). The foul contagion of rebellion is dispelled in such a way as to demonstrate Christ as the true epic champion. What no number of angels was able to accomplish, he manages effortlessly: he is, therefore, a hero *sui generis*.

> Yet half his strength he put not forth, but check'd
> His Thunder in mid Volley, for he meant
> Not to destroy, but root them out of Heav'n:
> The overthrown he rais'd, and as a Herd
> Of Goats or timorous flock together throng'd
> Drove them before him Thunder-struck. . . .
>
>   Hell heard th'unsufferable noise, Hell saw
> Heav'n ruining from Heav'n, and would have fled
> Affrighted; but strict Fate had cast too deep
> Her dark foundations, and too fast had bound.
> Nine days they fell; confounded *Chaos* roar'd,
> And felt tenfold confusion in their fall
> Through his wild Anarchy, so huge a rout
> Incumber'd him with ruin: (VI. 853-858, 867-874)

Not only is Heaven cleansed of the disorder momentarily intruded by Lucifer —the reach of chaos presumably never having been greater than it was before that epic resolution—but also, in words notable for their indirectness, we are assured that the anarch Chaos draws out for himself the grievous implications of that fall. Chaos has suffered injury, though Milton leaves the precise meaning of that injury quite to the reader's own imagination.

A second *chairos* follows necessarily upon the first since, as Milton constructs the cosmic history, the creation of the universe was the superabounding divine response to the decimation of Heaven. His God says

> But lest his heart exalt him in the harm
> Already done, to have dispeopl'd Heav'n,
> My damage fondly deem'd, I can repair
> That detriment, if such it be to lose
> Self-lost, and in a moment will create
> Another World.... (VII. 150-155)

That creation, in keeping with the biblical imagery of the world founded upon the "flood," is an order imposed upon a newly delimited and bounded Chaos. We are told how the Son of God took

> the golden Compasses, prepar'd
> In God's Eternal store, to circumscribe
> This Universe, and all created things:
> One foot he centred, and the other turn'd
> Round through the vast profundity obscure,
> And said, Thus far extend, thus far thy bounds,
> This be thy just Circumference, O World. (VII. 225-231)

The impact of this imposition upon Chaos is perhaps most readily seen in connection with the creative act of the second day. The Firmament is

> partition firm and sure,
> The waters underneath from those above
> Dividing: for as Earth, so he the World
> Built on circumfluous Waters calm, in wide
> Crystalline Ocean, and the loud misrule
> Of Chaos far remov'd, lest fierce extremes
> Contiguous might distemper the whole frame....

> (VII. 267-273)

Not just our earth, as the Genesis account implies, but for Milton the whole created order is divided by the Firmament's crystalline dome from the environing waters of chaos. The division described is a clean one, without opportunity for contamination. Once more the divine rule over chaos is unequivocally declared.

It is only at this point, however, with the appearance of man on the scene, that the issue of theodicy becomes truly germane. It is the threat posed by flux and evil to man's world that theodicy is designed to explain, and in the third *Chairos*, the covenant with Noah following upon the Flood, we are advised that certain disruptions of nature will in fact never recur. In the Genesis narrative, the Flood is plainly presented as a return of the world to the conditions of chaos; the fountains of the Deep are broken open, the protecting dome above is breached, and the "circumfluous" waters overwhelm man's domain. As Milton has Michael present this future history to Adam,

45

the emphasis falls upon the assurance that never again will chaos be permitted such intrusion:

> Such grace shall one just Man find in his sight,
> That he relents, not to blot out mankind,
> And makes a Cov'nant never to destroy
> The Earth again by flood, nor let the Sea
> Surpass his bounds, nor Rain to drown the World
> With Man therein or Beast.... (XI. 890-895)

The Rainbow marks the divine promise that certain regularities will persist: "Day and Night, / Seed-time and Harvest, Heat and hoary Frost" until divine fire purges all things new.

A fourth in this series of crucial events is the Nativity of Christ as Milton images it in his ode written a few days after his twenty-first birthday. The banishing of the demonic oracles provides much of the business of the poem, and while that is in itself clearly an ameliorating action, the axial event Milton gives us in Stanza XVIII. There he sums up with eight lines that mysterious salvation-history in which, whatever the appearances, evil suffers decisive setbacks and the total context of the human career is subtly transformed.

> And then at last our bliss
> Full and perfect is,
>   But now begins; for from this happy day
> Th'old Dragon under ground,
> In straiter limits bound,
>   Not half so far casts his usurped sway,
> And wroth to see his Kingdom fail,
> Swinges the scaly Horror of his folded tail.

The circumscribed Satan is here identified with the chthonic powers, certainly an evocative equation even if an untypical one for Milton. Since in Milton's scheme man's universe was not created until after Satan's banishment to Hell, Milton is not free as Dante was to associate Satan from the beginning with the underworld. Indeed, when we consider Dante's Satan immobilized in the depths of the Inferno we must admit that Milton's fallen angels enjoy an extraordinary freedom to travel. The circumscription which Milton describes in the ode foreshadows the action he later develops in *Paradise Regained*, and in these cases, as indeed with all in the series, we are to understand that divine omnipotence progressively overcomes evil.

That this overcoming of evil is also to be understood as an altering of the conditions upon human action is undoubtedly most clearly expressed in the argument of *Paradise Regained*. Between Old and New Testaments, the symbolic representation of the primary locus of evil underwent a significant development, and this is reflected in Milton's two epics. Between the time of *Paradise Lost* and that of *Paradise Regained*, Satan shifts his headquarters from Pandemonium in Hell to "the middle region of thick air" in our planet's own atmosphere, a shift which reflects the New Testament's rich imaging of air both as the kingdom of evil and mischievous spirits, and as the secular climate of opinion hostile to faith and virtue. To speak, as Milton does, of a cleansing of the air in *Paradise Regained* is to draw out with precise pictorial logic the claim that divine action alters the conditions influencing choice. I shall want to return to this point and expand it after noting the two final *chairoi* in Milton's sequence.

Christ's resurrection is described in *Paradise Lost*, XII. 422-433:

> the Stars of Morn shall see him rise
> Out of his grave, fresh as the dawning light,
> Thy ransom paid, which Man from death redeems,
> His death for Man, as many as offer'd Life
> Neglect not, and the benefit embrace
> By faith not void of works: this God-like
> Annuls thy doom, the death thou shouldst have di'd,
> In sin for ever lost from life; this act
> Shall bruise the head of *Satan*, crush his strength
> Defeating Sin and Death, his two main arms,
> And fix far deeper in his head thir stings
> Than temporal death shall bruise the Victor's heel.

Again, we are to suppose a curtailing of Satan; here his arms, Sin and Death, are robbed of strength. If these words are to have any meaning at all, it must be that the outpouring of divine grace in Christ's victory makes the virtuous —and felicitous—life markedly more attainable. The conditions have been altered.

Finally, as the climactic act in God's last judgment, Satan will be cast into the bottomless pit, the event all these other *chairoi* foreshadow and, in part, secure. For this Judgment, as the Nativity Ode pictures the event, "The dreadful Judge in middle Air shall spread his throne." The site is utterly appropriate, since the Last Judgment is nothing less than the final act in the transformation of those conditions on human choosing which, for the spiritual combat, are summed up as the poisoned atmosphere of the age. God's placing his throne in the middle air denotes his thorough supplanting of evil in that sector.

This line of thought has its fullest development in *Paradise Regained*. By Christ's success in meeting temptation, Eden is raised in the waste wilderness, and the atmosphere at least symbolically cleansed. That Milton should follow Luke's order for the temptations, in which Christ's confrontation of Satan on the pinnacle of the temple comes last, rather than Matthew's, in which that temptation comes second, is a choice readily appreciated once we explicate a central line of imagery in the poem.

Satan and his hosts ensconced in Earth's atmosphere celebrate there an usurped rule over the spiritual climate of man's world. This symbolic representation of the conditions which compromise human action is firmly rooted in New Testament imagery. Heinrich Schlier observes:

> In the Epistle to the Ephesians 2:2, "the prince of this world" is called "the prince of the power of the air". This strange name implies that the air is the medium in which his power is exercised. St. Paul is here in line with ancient tradition, particularly the statements of late Judaism. But what does he mean by "the air"? Paul himself provides the answer to this question: he explains that it is "the spirit that now worketh on the children of unbelief"—that is, or men who have rejected the Gospel. . . . But what is this spirit? In this context at least, it is the universal spirit of man's unbelief or disobedience. It is the general spiritual climate which influences mankind, in which men live, which they breathe, which dominates their thoughts, aspirations, and deeds. He exercises his "influence" over men by means of the spiritual atmosphere which he dominates and uses as the medium for his power. He gains power over men and penetrates them by means of this atmosphere which is his realm, the realm of his power.[11]

In the Renaissance this identification of the demonic with that worldly climate stultifying to faith and good works was further underlined by making the abode of demons identical with the middle regions of air where most weather was supposed to originate. So, not surprisingly, Satan in *Paradise Regained* is able to command a violent storm on the eve of the last temptation. The resonances here are profound, for the association of dragon (=Leviathan, Satan) with weather is all but universal. G. Elliot Smith provides a summary judgment: the dragon

> controls the rivers or seas, dwells in pools or wells, or in the clouds on the tops of mountains, regulates the tides, the flow of streams, or the rainfall, and is associated with thunder and lightning.[12]

Christ's adversary, then, sums up those contaminants which sully this world as an arena of free and virtuous action. That Christ's last temptation concludes with his standing balanced on the spire of the temple is to mark out the contrast between what lies within him and what lies without. Within, he is all equanimity, his "inner weather" under perfect control, unlike Adam's and Eve's after their fall when

> They sat them down to weep, nor only Tears
> Rain'd at thir Eyes, but high Winds worse within
> Began to rise.   (IX. 1121-1123)

Opposed to Christ's equanimity is Satan's dramatic collapse in his preempted airy element. He is likened to Antaeus "Throttl'd at length in th'Air" and to the Sphinx casting herself down from the heights. His defeat must mean that the atmosphere has been somehow cleansed, a hint of which surfaces when angels arrive to succour Christ, and bear him "As on floating couch through the blithe Air."

The final cleansing of the air, however, remains more as sure promise than as accomplished fact. The angelic chorus sings at the close:

> But thou, Infernal Serpent, shalt not long
> Rule in the Clouds; like an Autumnal Star
> Or Lightning thou shalt fall from Heav'n trod down
> Under his feet: for proof, ere this thou feel'st
> Thy wound, yet not thy last and deadliest wound
> By this repulse receiv'd. . . .   (IV. 618-623)

The apocalyptic defeat is yet to come, though one more battle has now been won. Seeing the redemptive public career of Christ as inaugurated by his baptism and meeting of temptation, Milton can speak of Eden recovered by these obscure events, far from the public eye. Perhaps Milton's unwillingness to claim more for this *chairos*, insofar as the cleansing of the air is concerned, stems from his awareness of arguments like that of St. Athanasius, which reserved such a victory for the crucifixion.

> If the devil, the enemy of our race, having fallen from heaven, wanders about our lower atmosphere, and there bearing rule over his fellow-spirits, as his peers in disobedience, not only works illusions by their means in them that are deceived, but tries to hinder them that are going up; while the Lord came to cast down the devil, and clear the air and prepare the way for us up into heaven—well, by what other kind of death could this have come to pass, than by one which took place in the air, I mean, the cross? For only he that is perfected on the cross dies in the air. Whence it was quite fitting that the Lord suffered this death. For thus being lifted up, he cleared the air of the malignity both of the devil and of demons of all kinds.[13]

In any case, this regaining of Eden is to be accepted as some radical alteration of the atmosphere enveloping human action.

It is significant for an understanding of Milton's meliorism to remember that in his biblical sources the apocalyptic defeat of Satan is followed by his everlasting consignment to the bottomless pit (or the abyss of the Lake of

Fire, as contrasted with the chthonic Hades or Sheol). Though this consignment, in Milton's chronology, had occurred not as an *eschaton* but as an event immediately prior to the opening of Book I of *Paradise Lost*, we may infer that in the final divine dispensation as Milton sees it Satan's wide ranging through chaos and cosmos will be altogether curtailed, with Satan exiled to the Lake of Fire once again.

The biblical symbols that bear on this point are rich indeed and while Milton does not explicitly work out their meaning, that meaning is latent in his presentation both of earth's marriage to heaven, and of cosmic meliorism. Balancing the figure of Satan sealed off in the bottomless pit (i.e., the abyss in its threatening aspect) is the figure of the River of Life (the abyss in its positive aspect) issuing from beneath the throne of God at the center of the eternal city. This motif is present in the prophecies of both Ezekiel and St. John the Divine, and indeed has a close counterpart in the Muslim tradition claiming that under God's throne there lies a sea of green water with which he quickens the dead.[14] In all these cases we would seem to have a variant of the fountain of Eden, but with an important increment of meaning: the abyssal has been brought under a more immediate divine surveillance and control.

So, while the abyssal is certainly not eradicated, it is perpetuated in two modes, so neatly divorced the one from the other that we must suppose the nature of choosing to be forever altered, a conclusion to which the whole thrust of Milton's cosmic meliorism leads. In the apocalyptic resolution, no longer will the conditions upon choosing be compromising and perverting. Rather they will define the freedom and openness of the eternal life. The promise is of everlasting novelty, but without risk.

Even as I suggest this formulation of how Milton's meliorism in fact helps to define ideal process, I realize how paradoxical and elusive the notion is. We confront in history ahead the same insoluble problem every human imagination has faced in picturing paradise behind: how does one escape the rule of contraries? If the Milton of *Areopagitica* is accurate, the full truth must ever lie beyond the grasp of a fallen and dialectical consciousness.

CHAPTER THREE

Herrick and Marvell:
The Paradisal Quest

Milton was by no means alone in his working out of new images for the paradisal in the 17th-century milieu. The English poets contemporary with him—especially Robert Herrick, Henry Vaughan, Andrew Marvell and Thomas Traherne—engaged the same problem on a number of fronts. Louis Martz, indeed, takes the prose meditations of Traherne as one of the two supreme representations in English literature (*Paradise Lost* is, of course, the other), and he can find a strikingly similar expression of Augustinian method and concern in the poetry of Vaughan.[1] If Herrick and Marvell are omitted in Martz's discussion of the paradise within, it is not because they do not treat of paradise at least as insistently as does Vaughan, but rather because their approaches are not so patently Augustinian. Meditative regimen is given little scope by either Herrick or Marvell, and in the discussion following I shall suggest how for these poets the appropriate categories of analysis are those developed above in the discussion of Milton.

In their accommodation of openness in the imaging of paradise, Herrick and Marvell are at antipodes. Herrick resolutely affirms the enclave, while Marvell with equal thoroughness affirms the open way. Though I shall have rather more to say about Marvell below, I do not intend Herrick to be seen merely as a foil. His vision signally evokes the particular aspirations any paradise must address. In these two poets' conjugate approaches to the paradisal quest we may find corroboration of Milton's position. The heavenly life as the career of regenerate man is a course which acknowledges both heaven and the Deep.

3.1   Herrick and the Search for Secure Space

Herrick's choice of title—*Hesperides*—for his volume of lyrics published in 1648 would, perhaps, be reason enough to include him in a treatment of paradise in the Age of Milton. The title delicately asserts for each of the lyrics included a link with the classical milieu's closest analogue to Eden: those sun-bathed isles of the West where golden apples are guarded by a dragon.

Yet I am here more particularly concerned with the collection of devotional poems, his *Noble Numbers*, which Herrick gathered at the end of *Hesperides*.

The *Noble Numbers* share with the secular lyrics those several features we find distinctive in Herrick's vision: his claustrophilia, as Morse Peckham has described the poet's inveterate fondness for proximate and secure places; the companion terror of all things uncharted and immeasurable; the fondness for the diminutive, whether insects in amber, flowers in crystal, or the infant Christ in his swaddling clothes; the incantatory vein; the mixing of classical and Christian motifs which H. W. Swardson and Cleanth Brooks, among others, have remarked.[2]

After considering Milton's concessions to the abyss in the presentation of his paradisal garden, and of his versions of paradise more amenable to process, it must be with some surprise that we discover how insistent Herrick is in associating paradise with the secure sanctuary, with any role for the abyss categorically denied. It seems likely that the assertiveness of the womb-like sanctuary in Herrick's *Noble Numbers* (as in the *Hesperides* at large) represents Herrick's peculiar response to the secularizing of space in his century, and—a point more easily demonstrated—his accommodation of a strangely troubled conscience.

To bring into focus Herrick's claustrophilia, no poem serves better than his "A Thanksgiving to God, for his House." The lyric opens:

> Lord, Thou hast given me a cell
> Wherein to dwell;
> A little house, whose humble roof
> Is weather-proof;
> Under the sparres of which I lie
> Both soft, and drie;
> Where Thou my chamber for to ward
> Hast set a Guard
> Of harmless thoughts, to watch and keep
> Me, while I sleep.[3]

This snug place, we learn with curiosity quickened, is apparently haven against more than the elements. The speaker is happy to have a "Guard / Of harmlesse thoughts," whatever they may shield him against. "His wish to God" sharpens the suggestion of "A Thanksgiving": the longing for an intimate and secure space is in fact for the womb-like sanctuary where consciousness will suffer a diminution:

> I would to God, that mine old age might have
> Before my last, but here a living grave,

> Some one poore Almes-house; there to lie, or stir,
> Ghost-like, as in my meaner sepulcher   *(Poems,* p . 393)

Here the womb-like space is also plainly the tomb, and its safety is that of carefully circumscribed life, rather than its trustful amplification. The emphasis throughout is upon reduction, diminishing:

> A little piggin, and pipkin by,
> To hold things fitting my necessity.

The delightful diminutives here—"piggin" and "pipkin"—remind us of Herrick's genius in speaking of the tiny. Elsewhere he had urged:

> God! to my little meale and oyle,
> Add but a bit of flesh, to boyle:
> And Thou my Pipkinnet shall see;
> Give a wave-offring unto Thee.   *(Poems,* p. 400)

That "Pipkinnet," being a little, *little* pot, surely has the dimensions of a teacup. The total effect is to persuade the reader that Herrick would, if he could, shrink the whole world to miniature and manageable proportions.

Such a "Ghost-like" condition, characterized by the diminutive and the familiar, and the guard of "harmlesse thoughts" is, we must conclude from the abundant evidence of the poetic context, above all else a haven from conscience. In "To his Conscience," Herrick had asked:

> Can I not sin, but thou wilt be
> My private *Protonotarie?*
>   . . .
> And wilt not thou, with gold, be ti'd
> To lay thy pen and ink aside?
> That in the mirk and tongueless night,
> Wanton I may, and thou not write?
> It will not be.   *(Poems,* p. 378)

Bad conscience, we must suppose, is implicated in his chronic insomnia. "To his angrie God" opens:

> Through all the night
> Thou doest me fright,
> and hold'st mine eyes from sleeping.   *(Poems,* p. 374)

Again, writing of the Last Judgment, Herrick says:

> Teares, at that day, shall make but weake defence;
> When Hell and Horrour fright the Conscience.
> Let me, though late, yet at the last, begin
> To shun the least Temptation to a sin.   *(Poems,* p. 416)

With that adjustment of conduct he shall find himself finally "safe in death." But the remainder of the poem leaves in doubt his success in acting upon such an exhortation to himself. The presiding impression given by his numerous discussions of conscience is that he cannot long refrain from frightening self-accusation. In "The Summe, and the Satisfaction," he tells us:

> Last night I drew up mine Account,
> And found my Debits to amount
> To such a height, as for to tell
> How I sho'd pay, 's impossible.   (*Poems*, p. 391)

While it is probably idle to speculate on the causes for Herrick's troubled conscience, the fact remains that the joy and sensuousness so often discussed under the rubric of Herrick's assumed paganism has its counterweight in this unease of mind. Herrick's wedding of pagan and Christian elements would appear to be a union not without its complications for the man behind the masks.

The motif of a truncated awareness, a living death in which conscience no longer plagues him, receives its definitive presentation in a poem appearing near the close of the *Noble Numbers*. "To his Saviours Sepulcher: his Devotion" begins with the curious apostrophe: "Haile holy, and all-honour'd Tomb, / By no ill haunted." So early in the devotion, the speaker must assure himself, no less than his reader, that the tomb is free of all spiritual threats. "How sweet this place is!" he goes on,

> as from hence
> Flow'd all *Panchaia's* Frankincense;
> Or rich *Arabia* did commix,
> Here, all her rare *Aromaticks*.

But what could have prepared us fully for the turn which his devotion then takes?

> Let me live ever here, and stir,
> No one step from this *Sepulcher*.
> Ravisht I am!   and down I lie,
> Confus'd, in this brave Extasie.

The fact of his confusion is a revelation, for it implies that the compulsion to seek out such sepulchral refuges is little understood by any of Herrick's speakers who so give image to desire.

The equation between paradise and tomb is then completed.

> Here let me rest; and let me have
> This for my *Heaven*, that was Thy *Grave*:

54

> And, coveting no higher sphere,
> I'le my Eternitie spend here.   (*Poems*, p. 426)

This compulsion so vividly realized here has had its transparent explanation in others of the *Noble Numbers*. The retreat to the womb-tomb is in fact the flight from conscience.

Given Herrick's predilection for the secure space, and the evidence for troubled conscience, we would expect to find certain features prominent in his imaging of hell and of paradise, and our expectation is not disappointed. Hell and abyss are identified, while paradise is a sanctuary in which an eternal spiralling in upon the divine center is guaranteed.

Of the nearly 300 poems collected as *Noble Numbers*, some 120 are couplet-epigrams. Most of the latter, it is true, are bromides in the vain of:

> God is not onely said to be
> An *Ens*, but *Supraentitie*.   (*Poems*, p. 360)

But his epigram on Hell, by virtue of its context, carries a considerable charge of meaning:

> Hell is no other, but a soundlesse pit,
> Where no one beame of comfort peeps in it.   (*Poems*, p. 394)

A fathomless pit—what other image could convey half as much terror for Herrick?

The counterpart-epigram, on the paradisal, runs:

> Paradise is (as from the Learn'd I gather)
> *A quire of blest Soules circling in the Father.*   (*Poems*, p. 406)

One suspects that here is a circle of zero-radius, with the blest in utter safety, having their movement in the very Center of all things. In his somewhat longer lyric "On Heaven," Herrick amplifies the conception. His request at the opening is remarkable: "Permit mine eyes to see / Part, or the whole of Thee [i.e., Heaven]." But then such audacity was commonplace, as we have seen, in reformed heavenly-mindedness. "O happy place!" Herrick continues,

> Where all have Grace,
> And Garlands shar'd,
> For their reward;
> Where each chast Soule
> In long white stole,
> And Palmes in hand,
> Do ravisht stand;
> So in a ring,
> The praises sing
> Of Three in One.   (*Poems*, p. 391)

The dynamics of the heavenly reality are left undeveloped, perhaps because some kind of stasis seems inseparable from beatitude as Herrick conceives of it. He is not capable of moving far beyond the comforts of the "living grave."

And yet, though his presiding imagery of paradise as womb-like security is decidedly regressive, Herrick's genius is sufficient to produce at least one poem in which the obsession with conscience is nearly overcome, and some intimation of paradise's ongoing transaction with the deep is provided to titillate the reader. I refer to "The white Island: or place of the Blest." In taking the measure of Herrick's achievement here I suggest his limited success in engaging the same issues which evoked such a rich response from Milton.

His first stanza serves to summarize much of the content of the *Noble Numbers*:

> In this world (*the Isle of Dreams*)
> While we sit by sorrowes streames,
> Teares and terrors are our theames
>   Reciting. (*Poems*, p. 399)

Can he, we wonder, go on to image a Heavenly Albion which is at the same time terror-free and lively, unlike those sundry sepulchral sanctuaries he has offered elsewhere? Terror-free it certainly is:

> There no monstrous fancies shall
> Out of hell an horrour call,
> To create (or cause at all)
>   Affrighting.

If the poet's fancy has, on earth, been afflicted or deranged, such cannot be the case in the place of the Blest. But how shall we understand the stanza which follows?

> There in calm and cooling sleep
> We our eyes shall never steep;
> But eternall wash shall keep,
>   Attending
>
> Pleasures, such as shall pursue
> Me immortaliz'd, and you;
> And fresh joyes, as never too
>   Have ending.

True, that eternal watch is spent attending to heavenly pleasures, as the poem concludes the matter. Yet the notion of eternal wakefullness, of a heavenly watch, contrasted with "calm and cooling sleep," has an undertow of meaning. It would appear that the speaker here cannot stretch his imagination to include a felicity which does not incorporate vigilance as its condition.

Therein, paradox though it may be, lies the peculiar strength and success of this poem. Earlier he had instructed us that death was a matter of "More and more approaching nigh / Unto young Eternitie." It is that youthfulness of "Eternitie," coupled with the "fresh joyes" of the penultimate line which directs our attention to an unusual dimension in this poem: the paradisal incorporates both novelty and growth. And even though the speaker is pursued by pleasures, rather than himself taking the initiative in their enjoyment, his watchful attending to them is to be seen as involving greater alertness than we find honored in his many poems on the womb-tomb.

In short, the speaker's watchfulness is double-edged. Though it cannot but remind the reader of the anxious vigilance of other poems, it also argues a fuller consciousness than Herrick was able to accommodate elsewhere.

There is, as well, a charming audacity in making Heaven a New Albion. While it assuredly associates Heaven with those other garden-island-enclaves proved wanting in the early decades of Milton's century, it also claims for Heaven that incorporation and transfiguration of historical particulars (Albion) which Milton too affirms in his vision of consummated finitude, Earth's marriage with Heaven.

If, finally, Herrick's efforts to image an earthly sanctuary altogether proof against threat and anxiety do not prosper, it must be that no earthly haven is any less vulnerable than Milton dared show his Edenic garden to be. Safety, while man is enfleshed, is a matter of the mind, making its own depths a heaven or hell; and Herrick's consciousness, we must infer, was too profoundly troubled to permit him to explore at greater length the model of the paradisal way.

3.2 Dialectic and Pilgrimage

While Herrick is the celebrant of enclaves, Andrew Marvell is the celebrant of the paradisal journey. The human career for him is a relentless pressing beyond limits, and enclaves, though not to be avoided, invariably pose the threats of artificiality, paralysis, and death. Yet, open as it is, man's career is a pilgrimage. Marvell's dialectic may prescribe the transcending of all manner of delights momentarily identified with by speaker and reader-auditor, but the goal of eternal joy is never in doubt. His work, then, is to be seen as yet another grappling during the Age of Milton with the imaging of felicity, his special contribution being the ordering and judging of his profound experience of the green world by appeal to the paradigm of Christian pilgrimage.

Though he is iconoclastic, often exasperatingly removed from his speakers, and ambiguous to a fault, his achievement in imaging a version of ideal process is a significant part of the story I am detailing.

The last generation of scholarship on Marvell's "green world," ably, if not exhaustively, summarized by Jim Swan in a recent article,[4] has performed two useful tasks: it has, at the hands of Frank Warnke, William Empson, Rosalie Colie, Louis Martz, Joseph Summers, and Swan himself, brought into clear focus the vexatious issue of tone; Marvell is seen to be detached, playful, ambivalent—so much so that what the poet believes on any issue is most elusive; but also, at the hands of Ruth Wallerstein, Ann Berthof and Milton Klonsky, among others, Marvell's indebtedness to a host of intellectual traditions—Platonic, neo-Platonic, Hermetic, Patristic—has been explicated.

Typically, the learning brought to bear in this second approach does not do justice to the playfulness of the poet, and I must add, in qualification of Swan's summary position, that those who stress Marvell's ironic ambivalence do not do full justice to that theme of Christian wayfaring which runs through his lyrics. The choice that Swan offers, for example, is between ironic play and the poet's flight into transcendence, neither of which makes adequate allowance for Marvell's commitment to this world. The possibility of a dialectical pilgrimage,[5] in which this world is carefully used in preparation for another, is not considered. I quote Swan's most relevant statements since they put so concisely this Hobson's choice.

> It cannot be overemphasized that it is largely through the ironic play with language and form, which is a manner appropriate to ambivalence, that Marvell maintains control [over the green world] rather than through the various possibilities of flight into transcendence available from Renaissance syncretism among Christian, Platonic, and Hermetic sources. This is especially true of "The Garden," which has been explained variously as a poem based either on the *Song of Solomon* or the *Enneads* or the *Pimander* or the *Meditations* of Descartes, to name only a few of the intellectual traditions claimed for the poem.[6]

Swan goes on to develop a judiciously psychoanalytic approach to Marvell's green world, which is faithful to Marvell's irony, at least, if not to his sources.

I wish to pursue here an inspiration which sees neither ironic ambivalence nor any of the peripheral intellectual movements of Marvell's time as the heart of Marvell's vision of nature. One can do justice to his irony by sketching out the several approaches to the green world which the poet presents dialectically—that is, approaches which are explored and set aside, but not without some truth extracted for later employment. I propose to show also that his vision of Christian pilgrimage in the green world is indeed a version of paradisal wayfaring conformable to that vision Milton offers at the close of *Paradise Lost* and again in *Paradise Regained*, where the career of obedience is seen to raise an *"Eden in the waste Wilderness."*

The dialogue which opens the 1681 *Poems* is, if anything, an over-statement of that resolution of soul which can be traced throughout the collection. The resolved soul is confronted with temptations for each sense and, in a marvellous show of intransigence, triumphs over the whole lot. Her "gentler Rest is on a Thought, / Conscious of doing what she ought."

To take this poem as a keynoting statement is not to deny the presence of hyperbole, which surfaces again conspicuously in the later "Dialogue between the Soul and Body." Yet the normative statement of the Chorus (of angels?), assuring the Soul, and the reader, that the Soul's true end lies beyond, is unimpeachable. I think the only possible way to accommodate the incisiveness of the Soul's rebuttals is to take them as substantially true. The function of the ironic hyperbole, then, is not to undermine the Soul's position but rather to suggest that she is not saying all that might be said. The awareness of the Soul, in this opening poem, is not sufficiently dialectical, a weakness which the ensuing poetry will more than remedy. She speaks, as it were, before rather than after experience, from *a priori* conviction rather than *a posteriori* wisdom. Like the Lady of *Comus*, or the resolved Christ of *Paradise Regained*, she meets temptation as if nothing of her own inwardness is manifest in the tempter. And this, of course, is to falsify the truth of temptation as psychomachia. Every man is tempted when he is drawn away by his own lust, and enticed, the epistle-writer James has insisted. Such a link between temptation and inner experience is lacking in the dramatic debate Marvell offers us. To put this another, and perhaps more helpful way: we do not see how the Resolved Soul can recognize or admit a good, perverted or abused, in each of the temptations, with which she is posed.

In examining the first of these temptations, I illustrate how later poetry in the collection elaborates the good to be dialectically explored in experience and show, more specifically, the first of the several approaches to the green world which Marvell judges in the light of Christian pilgrimage.

What Created Pleasure proposes to the Soul is, despite the freighted term "heighten," actually a version of mystical descent, a conjugation with fruits and flowers which Marvell will describe effectively in other poems. "Lay aside that Warlike Crest," Pleasure urges,

> And of Nature's banquet share:
> Where the Souls of fruits and flow'rs
> Stand prepar'd to heighten yours.[7]

59

Here, certainly, is hinted that empathy for the green world which, as one of Marvell's distinctive gifts, we would not expect to find the poet wholly repudiating. A modern reader, I suppose, could dismiss this temptation as the urging of the joys of inebriation, but Marvell's use of the term "souls" encourages us to pursue some less modern conceiving of the link between spiritous and spiritual. The link is readily documented, and it explains this and Marvell's other references to seduction by fruit.

In Renaissance lore, man's commerce with the green world was understood to include the possibility of a confluence of vegetable spirits with the human "spirit," or medial soul. Sir Kenelm Digby, it is true, sets forth this transaction in terms of the more familiar category of the human vital *spirits*:

> Within a living body, such as is mans, the intern spirits do aid, and contribute much facility to the spirits that are without, such as those of fruits are, to make their journey the more easie to the brain.[8]

But Timothy Bright in his *Treatise of Melancholy* (1586) made explicit the role of that mysterious third element in man construed as body, soul and spirit. The human spirit

> is a knot, to joyne both our soules and bodies together; so nothing of other nature can have corporall conjunction with us, except their spirites with ours first growe into acquaintance.[9]

Such "corporall conjunction," innocent enough as the eating and assimilation of fruits, yet carried the danger of the human spirit's becoming submerged among the lesser spirits of the green world. Ripened fruit, in which the spiritous elements most pleasing to man had gathered at the superficies[10] had, we are assured by Jacob Boehme, assumed "Venus's body."[11] In Marvell's "The Garden" the speaker re-enacts the Fall as he is beset by such ravishing fruits.

> The Nectaren, and curious Peach,
> Into my hands themselves do reach;
> Stumbling on Melons, as I pass,
> Insnar'd with Flow'rs, I fall on Grass. (37-40)

Yet, on two counts we are prevented from taking such seduction by fruit— such "heightening" of spirit by spirit—as altogether evil, whatever the position of the "Resolved Soul" in the opening dialogue. First ,"The Garden" as context for this occasion does not permit us to construe it as wholly negative. Plainly we have imaged here a consummate experience for the body, however partial that experience must be reckoned when juxtaposed, as it is, with those of mind and soul. Second, we have, in "Bermudas" a delectable couplet which presents such seduction by fruit as part of a paradisal vision in which God himself is seen as the tempter:

> He makes the Figs our mouths to meet;
> And throws the Melons at our feet.   (21-22)

Positive as such experiences may be, they are not to be lingered over; both "The Garden" and "Bermudas" close with pointed reminders of the temporal order in which man as wayfarer asserts his transcendence of the green world.

It seems likely, though neither fruit nor flower is involved, that we have a further illustration of the mystical descent in Marvell's description of the grove on the Appleton House estate.

> When first the Eye this Forrest sees
> It seems indeed as *Wood* not *Trees*:
> As if their Neighbourhood so old
> To one great Trunk them all did mold.
> There the huge Bulk takes place, as ment
> To thrust up a *Fifth Element*;
> And stretches still so closely wedg'd
> As if the Night within were hedg'd.   (St. LXIII)

The "green shade" is so dense here that it suggests the quintessence, or "*Fifth Element*." It happens that quintessence, in the Hermetic literature of the time, could mean among other things that medial soul or spirit which I alluded to earlier. More precisely, the quintessence was the unifying spirit of nature, both within and without man. So Henry Agrippa, after explaining how all things sublunary answer to counterparts in the other, more exalted realms of the celestial, intellectual and exemplary, indicates that the means of this correspondence is "that Celestiall power which they call the quintessence, or the spirit of the world, or the middle nature."[12] As "middle nature," the quintessence joined human soul with body, and both to the forms of all external things. The supposition that something of this meaning obtains for "quintessence" in this passage is borne out a few stanzas later when Marvell sums up his experience within the grove:

> Thus I, *easie Philosopher*,
> Among the *Birds* and *Trees* confer:
> And little now to make me, wants
> Or of the *Fowles*, or of the *Plants*.
> Give me but Wings as they, and I
> Streight floting on the Air shall fly:
> Or turn me but, and you shall see
> I was but an inverted Tree.   (St. LXII)

Beyond the light-hearted exhortations which acknowledge the limits of his body, the passage breathes the experience of participation in the lower forms of nature.

In "The Garden," we recall, the speaker had toyed with the ideas of Apollo's vegetable love for Daphne, and Pan's for Syrinx, but had himself taken the stance of the rational Adam in Eden, naming the plants, at least, if not the animals:

> Fair Trees!   where s'eer your barkes I wound,
> No Name shall but your own be found.

Here his identification with bird and plant, whatever its final seriousness, is complete. Such alterations of consciousness if we are to believe the "Created Pleasure" of the opening dialogue, are perhaps the strongest temptations to be offered the soul in pilgrimage, and Marvell is ever aware of their appeal. But to succumb, finally, to seduction by tree, fruit, or flower, is to suffer a dwindling of distinctions. A return to the abyssal state, by way of the vegetative order, is to suffer a diminution, rather than an enhancement of consciousness.

Beyond his critique of the mystical descent, Marvell's dialectical approach to the special joys of nature is evident also in his handling of the neo-Platonic motif of green thoughts and white. The "green thought" is that mentioned in the climactic stanza of "The Garden"; the "white and circling thoughts" of "On a Drop of Dew" provide the complement. Taken together, green thoughts and white comprise a vertical axis of neo-Platonic concerns—i.e., generation or generative thought, and contemplative recollection—which Marvell is careful to subordinate to the horizontal axis of Christian wayfaring. What is above and what is beneath are both to serve what is ahead, attained through the dialectic of experience.

The paradigm of the human soul at the heart of Plotinus' system is that of a bi-polar agency, involved in the two activities of contemplation and generation, and it seems probable that in this dichotomy we have the provenance for Marvell's richly imagined opposition of white and green. In his fifth Ennead Plotinus says:

> Soul arises out of the motionless Intellectual-Principle ... but the Soul's operation is not similarly motionless; its image is generated from its movement. It takes fulness by looking to its source; but it generates its image by adopting another, a downward movement.[13]

And the image so produced, he adds, is "Sense and Nature, the vegetal principle." Looking above itself, through all its hierarchically ordered "priors" back to the One, the contemplative Soul is able to generate another order

62

beneath itself. The proper harmonization of such "white" contemplation and "green" generation is nicely put by Dean Inge: "the more the Soul lives in the light of Spirit, 'turned towards' that which is above itself, the more creative it becomes, though its work is done with its back turned."[14] Yet there is constant peril in the soul's creative activity. Inge sums up Plotinus' understanding of the soul's idolatry: "the soul is perpetually constructing a synthesis out of what it has seen and apprehended; it is these premature syntheses which frequently have to be destroyed, or they will detain us in a world of shadows."[15] The ever-present temptation to the soul is to turn away from its priors, and become engrossed in the order of the created, to which she has herself richly contributed.

Now as Marvell dialectically presents this neo-Platonic scheme, it is not merely the descent into the "vegetable" order, whether through the seductions of fruit, or—as we shall see in a moment—the delights of creative thought, which stand under judgment. It is also the "white thought" of contemplative recollection. Let us explore these alternatives of green thought and white thought more fully.

In "The Garden," we recall, once the speaker has fallen prostrate upon the grass, his mind "Withdraws into its happiness." For Marvell the mind is assuredly anything but passive. True, it offers resemblance to everything outside it;

> Yet it creates, transcending these,
> Far other Worlds, and other Seas;
> Annihilating all that's made
> To a green Thought in a green Shade.   (II. 45-48)

This, we must suppose, is the mind's ultimate métier; limitlessly creative, able to create even "other Seas," or reservoirs of forms, it is also able to achieve an absolute and abstract generalization upon the created order it receives as data: the latter is itself a generative thought, *natura naturans*. Yet it must be noticed that the effect of "annihilating" is to criticize the mind's activity, and the pulling of the whole exhilirating expansion back to the limits of "green shade" is to suggest that Marvell does not wish to ally his estimate of the mind, finally, with those most liberal affirmations of Renaissance optimism. Paracelsus, for example, makes claims that at points remind us of Marvell, but clearly go beyond him. He declares:

> Thoughts are free and are subject to no rule. On them rests the freedom of man, and they tower above the light of nature. For thoughts give birth to a creative force that is neither elemental nor sidereal. . . . Thoughts create a new heaven, a new firmament, a new source of energy, from which new arts flow. . . . When a man undertakes to create something, he

establishes a new heaven, as it were, and from it the work that he desires to create flows into him. For such is the immensity of man that he is greater than heaven and earth.[16]

Marvell is content to speak of new worlds and seas, circumspectly omitting heaven from his reckoning. And I would add that by stressing greenness Marvell temperately affirms a link with the "elemental" which the more impetuous Paracelsus sets aside.

Yet the range of the mind here is vast indeed. That "The Garden" does not end with the couplet most readers, I suppose, would count as the primary touchstone of Marvell's work, says much about the larger concerns of the poem. For the soul has not yet realized its unique promise. In a memorable image we are told that it glides into the boughs,

> And, till prepar'd for longer flight,
> Waves in its Plumes the various Light.

The mention is so slight, it could be overlooked. The soul must *prepare* for her "longer flight." The several ecstasies of body, mind, and of the soul herself are, we are encouraged to believe, part but not the whole of that preparation. Their compounded felicity may be reminiscent of

> that happy Garden-state,
> While Man there walk'd without a Mate.

Yet the garden proves no place to dwell. The speaker returns to more ordinary reality by way of a flower clock which subtly asserts that every green and growing thing speaks of time. The garden-retreat here has clearly been "used." The world of time is the world of preparation. The reach of man's mental powers, and the long-range aspirations of his soul seem, for Marvell, to guarantee a pilgrimage which is endlessly dialectical.

The antitype of the green descent, whether through seduction by fruit or through green thoughts is, for Marvell, the white ascent of contemplative recollections which may exact a forgetfulness of this world as its price. His meditation "On a Drop of Dew" is, I admit, usually read as an endorsement of that upward movement. Like the dewdrop on the morning rose,

> the Soul, that Drop, that Ray,
> Of the clear Fountain of Eternal Day,
> Could it within the humane flow'r be seen,
> Remembring still its former height,
> Shuns the sweat leaves and blossoms green;
> And, recollecting its own Light,
> Does, in its pure and circling thoughts, express
> The greater Heaven in an Heaven less.   (19-26)

Platonic, or Neo-Platonic, motifs are all plain enough here: the soul's anamnesis, given that peculiar Plotinian turn of "pure and circling thoughts;" the soul's tension with the body, shunning the "sweat leaves and blossoms green;" and of course the notion of soul as light-source, so fully worked out by Boehme and the Cambridge Platonists.

But the Neo-Platonic regime of descent and return is a far remove from Christian pilgrimage, and the closing metaphors should be understood as qualifying the implications of earlier lines, leaving the reader with a notion of pilgrimage more world-affirming. For the soul, at the close, is compared not to dewdrop, but to manna:

> Such did the Manna's sacred Dew destil;
> White and intire, though congeal'd and chill.
> Congeal'd on Earth: but does, dissolving, run
> Into the Glories of th'Almighty Sun.

Moments earlier, the soul was the moisture-bead to be sublimed into the heavens by evaporation, but it has now, under the metaphor of manna, become the bread of heaven. It is true that the manna not consumed by the wayfaring Israelites was sublimed like the dew, but that was assuredly not the point of the divine provision. Manna was to be eaten, a dispensation for pilgrimage in the wilderness. And the body, clearly subordinated ten lines earlier, subtly re-asserts itself. The manna is an adjunct of pilgrimage.[17] While the soul may be likened to the dew, it is no contemplative flight from this world which is finally licensed.

In turning now to Marvell's use of occasional meditation, I consider an approach to nature no less dialectical than those I have just discussed, but one in which the benefits for the wayfarer are more conspicuous. The Christian's career in Marvell's time was often described in terms of a meditative regimen which attended to all the creatures of ordinary experience not as objects to be loved but as signposts to be read. Ruth Wallerstein has worked out the Catholic antecedents for such a regimen, and I have elsewhere documented the Puritan formulations.[18] Here I wish to show how for Marvell occasional meditation participates in the paradisal process of Christian pilgrimage.

As he prepares to leave the retreat of "The Garden," the speaker of that poem describes a flower sun dial, as I mentioned above, closing with a metaphor which evokes the commonplaces of occasional meditation:

> How well the skilfull Gardner drew
> Of flow'rs and herbes this Dial new;
> Where from above the milder Sun

Does through a fragrant Zodiack run;
And, as it works, the'industrious Bee
Computes its time as well as we.
How could such sweet and wholsome Hours
Be reckon'd but with herbs and flow'rs!

Behind the metaphor of the industrious bee is a voluminous literature insisting that all the occasions of experience might be redeemed by using them to yield light and sustenance. Thomas Adams, the eloquent Puritan preacher, speaks for the tradition in saying

> A good Christian, that like the Bee workes honey from every flower, suffers no action, demonstration, event, to slip by him without a question. All objects to a meditating *Solomon*, are like wings to reare and mount up his thoughts to Heaven.[19]

In Marvell's work the best sustained illustration of such meditative strategy is furnished by "Upon Appleton House",[20] Marvell's long poem on the country estate where he lived in the early 1650's tutoring Lord Fairfax's daughter Mary. This work has come to be seen as the crowning achievement in the genre of poems on country houses.

The poet's claims for the wisdom occasional meditation could draw from nature are perhaps most evident in a memorable stanza describing the grove on the Appleton estate.

Out of these scatter'd *Sibyls* Leaves
Strange *Prophecies* my Phancy weaves;
And in one History consumes,
Like *Mexique Paintings*, all the *Plumes*.
What *Rome, Greece, Palestine*, ere said
I in this *light Mosaick* read.
Thrice happy he who, not mistook,
Hath read in *Natures mystick Book*.   (St. LXXIII)

The *"light Mosaick,"* of course, involves a brilliant pun. Describing the checkerboard of light and shade beneath the boughs, the phrase in its primary sense points back to the "various Light" in which the soul-bird of "The Garden" waved its plumes. Marvell, it is certain, would not like Shelley speak of life "like a dome of many-coloured glass" staining the white radiance of Eternity, for all sense of staining is absent from Marvell's image. Precisely the mixture of light and shadow is what his speakers find delectable. Green shade epitomizes a finitude affirmed and delighted in. Yet this "light Mosaick" refers also to the Pentateuch, or Mosaic revelation; and the spokesman here could not make plainer the claim that all the wisdom of Scripture and the classical literatures is contained in this light sifting through the boughs of Appleton's grove.

The caveat, provided almost parenthetically in the closing line of the stanza, assumes in its brevity that the reader needs only the barest nudge to be reminded of how in fact nature yields her wisdom. To be "not mistook" is to avoid searching for any resting place in the natural world. Thrice happy the man who knows how to read nature's signposts. When, in the penultimate stanza, Marvell is most explicit about relating occasional meditation to paradise, it is in language assuring the wayfarer of guidance. Apostrophizing the estate, he exclaims: " 'Tis not, what once it was, the World," but rather a "rude heap," and hodge-podge of "Gulfes, Deserts, Precipices, Stone"; he continues:

> Your lesser *World* contains the same.
> But in more decent Order tame;
> *You Heaven's Center, Nature's Lap.*
> *And Paradice's only Map.*   (St. LXXXXVI)

The poet, we notice, is careful not to confuse the map with the territory. Furthermore, he implies that he has demonstrated how to "read" the Appleton estate so that it points the way to felicity.

An important part of that demonstration is the distance which, in the stanzas following the mention of "Nature's mystick Book," comes to separate Marvell from that "easie Philosopher" who has spoken for him through much of the poem. The "easie Philosopher" permits infatuation with the grove to cloud his judgment; but the price to be paid for lingering in the grove, and turning aside from wayfaring, is implicit in the imagery of crucifixion unqualified by the hope of resurrection.

The first hint of the distance widening between poet and speaker comes in Stanza LXXIV, when we learn that as oak leaves and ivy bedeck him, he moves "Like some great *Prelate of the Grove*." Though the phrase has antecedents enough in occasional meditation, where man often is described as priest offering the praises of the mute creation beneath him (cf. Herbert's "Providence"), the context here must render it ironic. The Puritan strictures upon prelacy cannot be ignored, when Cromwell's general Lord Fairfax and Marvell the Puritan apologist are both presences informing the Appleton estate.

No less ironic are the lines opening Stanza LXXV:

> Then, languishing with ease, I toss
> On Pallets swoln of Velvet Moss. . . .

The "ease" of the persona now takes on explicit links with languor, and more especially the unwillingness to leave the glade at all for the demanding world outside.

> How safe, methinks, and strong, behind
> These Trees have I encamp'd my Mind;
> Where beauty, aiming at the Heart,
> Bends in some Tree its useless Dart.

But the conditions for remaining in the grove are nothing less than a crucifixion by its green life:

> Bind me, ye *Woodbines* in your 'twines,
> Curle me about ye gadding Vines,
>
> . . .
>
> Do you, O *Brambles*, chain me too,
> And courteous *Briars* nail me through.

The import of such metaphors is too uncompromising to permit any but an ironic reading of the lines. It is consistent with the "easiness" of this philosopher that he could so lightly contemplate a vegetable crucifixion; this is the same figure who assured us he was all but indistinguishable from bird and from tree. But the distinction he cannot erase is that between speaker and Marvell himself. For the poet, this talk of remaining in the grove is folly—deftly and lightly described, it is true, but folly all the same. However much the grove may teach, it like garden and field must be left behind in the process of Christian pilgrimage.

3.3   Transcendence and Marvell's Green World

Mystical descent and green thought, we have seen, are judged by the canon of pilgrimage, while occasional meditation is shown by Marvell to be a natural support of Christian wayfaring; but is it possible to locate in the *Poems*, outside the opening dialogue which defines ends but leaves means obscure, an explicit description of that paradisal way which Marvell hints of, but seems determined only to hint?

I believe an affirmative answer may be given to the question, for in "Clorinda and Damon" we have, even if not in Marvell's own voice, a statement about Christian calling so explicit and so penetrating that the pastoral framework can accommodate it only by being transfigured. Regeneration and vocation, the primary reference of Milton's phrase "the Paradise within," are plainly imaged in the dialogue, as is the apprehension of the green world as one enjoyed most when subordinated to the divine. Before developing these points, I find it convenient to supply a frame for the poem by drawing upon Chapters One and Two above.

Milton's Eden, we recall, was transcended both by the waters of the Deep, and by God who walked there in the evening. The abyssal and heavenly orders so represented are readily understood as marking out the provisionality (or vulnerability) of Eden's Garden. In those two orders, we may suppose, were comprised the openness and the guarantees requisite for everlasting process; and Adam and Eve in exile, so long as they responded to the heavenly voice, had open to them a way in which the abyssal and heavenly were forever joined.

Now heavenly calling is evident enough in "Clorinda and Damon," but I think we shall only perceive how Marvell tacitly incorporates the abyssal in the closing unison celebration of "flowry Pastures" if we look first at two other poems from his hand. In "The Mower Against Gardens" and in the mower-passage of "Upon Appleton House," Marvell associates the grassy fields with the inexhaustible depths of nature but also, more significantly, with pilgrimage.

The Mower is one of the most provocative of Marvell's personae. As Geoffrey Hartman has shown, Marvell takes the static figure of the emblem-tradition and gives him life. In his diatribe against the stagnation and perversity of the garden, the Mower seems to be speaking one of Marvell's normative truths: the tendency of art is to remove terms from the dialectic of experience. So in "The Mower Against Gardens," as in "The Nymph Complaining," and "The Unfortunate Lover," the enclave of art provides as its enduring monuments figures incapable of movement. Art, we are advised, is never equal to the openness of life.

After a number of witty complaints about the hybrids of the garden, the Mower concludes:

> 'Tis all enforc'd; the Fountain and the Grot;
>   While the sweet Fields do lye forgot:
> Where willing Nature does to all dispence
>   A wild and fragrant Innocence:
> And *Fauns* and *Faryes* do the Meadows till,
>   More by their presence then their skill.
> Their Statues polish'd by some ancient hand,
>   May to adorn the Gardens stand:
> But howso'ere the Figures do excel,
>   The *Gods* themselves with us do dwell.   (31-40)

It is part of Marvell's audacity that he would here associate Mower and fields with "fragrant innocence," for in his love-complaints the Mower is clearly a casualty of adult experience. Yet the "sweet Fields" are finally to be seen as enjoying precisely that sort of fundamental ambiguity which characterizes the Deep: on the one hand, fathomless promise, scope, vitality, even "presence" which vivifies nature as skill cannot, and on the other hand, threat, condition and constraint. This second element we see more dramatically presented in the mower-section of "Upon Appleton House."

The speaker of that poem moves to the fields after he has meditated in the estate's garden upon the English Civil War and Lord Fairfax's choice to retire to the countryside.

> And now to the Abyss I pass
> Of that unfathomable Grass,
> Where Men like Grashoppers appear,
> And Grashoppers are Gyants there: (369-372)

Immediately we are located, not only in an infinitely promising expanse like that which receives the speaker of "The Garden" after his seduction by fruit, but also in the milieu of Israel in pilgrimage, for the allusion is to Kadesh-Barnea and the ten spies' report that they felt themselves to be grasshoppers in the eyes of the natives of the promised land (Numbers 13:31-33).

Designated as "Abyss," and offering flowers to those who descend into its depths (383-384), the grass becomes a charged image of regenerative possibilities. But Marvell is not content with images of descent and re-ascent, even when they promise renewal. I quote in full his stanza on the mowers, for the figure sums up a most significant relationship between pilgrimage and the world of experience:

> No scene that turns with Engines strange
> Does oftner then these Meadows change.
> For when the Sun the Grass hath vext,
> The tawny Mowers enter next;
> Who seem like Israelites to be,
> Walking on foot through a green Sea.
> To them the Grassy Deeps divide,
> And crowd a Lane to either side.

These "Grassy Deeps" imply the same judgment upon the world of experience that we discussed above in connection with Milton's meliorism. We recall that the "Grassy Deeps" of Jesus' parables and of *Areopagitica* referred to the fundamentally ambiguous conditions upon work and choice in this world. Wheat and tares grow confusedly together, and that jumble is, in the submerged mythical logic of biblical poetry, identical with the ambiguity of the watery deep as context for human action.

That this "Grassy Deep" is indeed to be understood as imaging the folds of "dire necessity" like those in which Milton's Samson became entangled is made clear in the following stanza:

> With whistling Sithe, and Elbow strong,
> These Massacre the Grass along:
> While one, unknowing, carves the *Rail*,
> Whose yet unfeather'd Quils her fail.
> The Edge all bloody from its Breast
> He draws, and does his stroke detest;
> Fearing the Flesh untimely mow'd
> To him a Fate as black forebode.   (393-400)

One intends, but effects both more and less than he intended. Furthermore, these "tawny Mowers," so plainly identified with the tragedy and travail of adult experience, "seem like *Israelites*." The biblical poems on the crossing of the Red Sea had forever fixed the Red Sea as a finger of the Deep. (Cf. for example, Exodus 15 and Psalm 106:8-11). Yet, for his pilgrim people, God subdues all threatening possibilities. That Marvell wishes us, finally, to see the grassy wilderness as an equivalent setting for pilgrimage is strongly hinted in the close of the following stanza when Thestylis, the cook for the band of mowers, seizes another bird and cries that God

> call'd us *Israelites*;
> But now, to make his saying true
> Rails rain for Quails, for Manna Dew.   (406-408)

The "Abyss" of the grass yields both flowers, and food; and yet it offers no abiding place. To capitalize this point, Marvell concludes the episode with a description of the meadow's actual flooding.

> Then to conclude these pleasant Acts,
> *Denton* sets ope its *Cataracts*;
> And makes the Meadow truly be
> (What it but seem'd before) a Sea.

We may see how, in his several presentations of Mower and mowers, Marvell is honest to the ambiguity of the "Grassy Deeps." Nature may be fathomless, but man can take no sure hope in that knowledge, since that fathomlessness means infinite possibility for pain, loss, and wandering. Only as the Deep is joined with heavenly calling is pilgrimage possible. Christian wayfaring takes place in the context of a fathomless world, but in response to altogether specific directives. This, finally, is the wisdom conveyed by the body of Marvell's lyrics, but the truth is epitomized in "Clorinda and Damon."

This poem appears seventh from the opening in the 1681 edition of Marvell's lyrics. While we cannot be positive that the ordering is Marvell's own, it is fair to say that the opening group which ends with "Clorinda and Damon" fixes a firmly Christian tonality for the entire collection. First in that group is "A Dialogue between the Resolved Soul and Created Pleasure," which rigorously establishes goods "that lie beyond the Pole" as the proper pursuit of the soul. "On a Drop of Dew" and its Latin version, "Ros," iterate that message. "The Coronet" is Marvell's most explicit critique of his art by the canons of Christian faith. Bringing to Christ a coronet, he finds

> the Serpent old
> That, twining in his speckled breast,
> About the flow'rs disguis'd does fold,
> With wreaths of Fame and Interest.

Then we have "Eyes and Tears" with its celebration of Christian pentience. The speaker there assures us:

> I have through every Garden been,
> Amongst the Red, the White, the Green;
> And yet, from all the flow'rs I saw
> No Hony, but these Tears could draw.

Immediately preceding "Clorinda and Damon," comes Marvell's celebration of the Atlantic paradise in "Bermudas." "Clorinda and Damon" has, I believe, a religious explicitness in keeping with that of these half-dozen poems which precede it.[21]

The exchange opens with Clorinda's encouraging Damon to join her in a love-retreat "Where *Flora* blazons all her pride." When Damon refuses, she points to another place: "Seest thou that unfrequented Cave?" But Damon refuses again, calling it a den and virtue's grave. Clorinda goes on to describe the delights of the fountain nearby, but Damon poses the question:

> Might a Soul bath there and be clean,
> Or slake its Drought?

When Clorinda inquires after his meaning, he explains:

> These once had been enticing things,
> *Clorinda*, Pastures, Caves and Springs.

But he has recently met Pan. "What did great *Pan* say," Clorinda asks, and Damon answers:

> Words that transcend poor Shepherds skill.
> But He ere since my Songs does fill:
> And his Name swells my slender Oate.

After the two speakers agree that Pan would sound sweetly in either's voice, they join in a chorus.

> Of *Pan* the flowry Pastures sing,
> Caves eccho, and the Fountains ring,
> Sing then while he doth us inspire;
> For all the World is our *Pan's* Quire.

If we assume, as seems natural, that the Damon of this early poem is one and the same with Damon the Mower whom we encounter later, then Damon's pointed turning aside from "Pastures, Caves and Springs" is an inclusive and anticipatory critique of later positions. The "Caves," as enclaves of love, are rejected, though they are more natural retreats than that of the Garden; but more important, "Pastures" and "springs," two images evocative of abyssal depth both in Marvell and in the traditions we have examined above, are no "enticing things." Not, at least, after Damon's encounter with Pan. Yet, in the concluding chorus, pastures, caves and fountains are all affirmed as they testify of Pan.

This chorus, it happens, represents the only occasion in Marvell's dialogues when the conversants join in unison at the close, and the concert of voices is surely significant. Not only is the unison of nature's praise the subject of the chorus, but the transcendent all-subsuming truth of Damon's message is underlined by his and Clorinda's reconciliation. Whether or not, as Louis Martz seems to doubt,[22] Clorinda has imbibed all of Damon's meaning, she has assuredly accepted both his terms and his uncompromising piety. To worship Pan is to pursue a devotion that transcends "poor Shepherds skill"— i.e., that puts all one's art under judgment and, at the same time, paradoxically, fills it wholly.

Such momentous claims are scarcely to be laughed aside, even if joyousness defines the tone of the closing chorus. The poem is best read, I believe, as putting and answering a question which probes the limits of pastoral. For Marvell the pastoral world is to be understood as perfected in Pan's choir, with every part uttering the praise of Christ, and so sustaining pilgrimage. To live in a complete obedience to the words of Pan, we may suppose, would mean an ever-sustained joy like that which the closing chorus both describes and expresses. Such is a paradisal way.

A close analogy, then, holds between Marvell's pilgrimage in the fathomless green world and Milton's "*Eden* rais'd in the waste Wilderness." Each is plainly not a public vision; each involves a transfiguration of wilderness by the perception of the way to be travelled through it. In each, paradise becomes a matter of finitude rectified, of process immediately if not finally or totally reconciled with the ideal.

A difficult question remains for us to consider in closing: given the nature of the paradisal quest as set forth in the Age of Milton, what and where is man's *home*? For both Marvell and Milton open process makes the very idea of an enduring resting place problematic. Matching Marvell's dialectical vision of enclave and way is Milton's expansive view of a human destiny never limited to a single realm. We remember Raphael's conjecture—surely not altogether idle—made to Adam:

> Your bodies may at last turn all to spirit,
> Improved by tract of time, and wing'd ascend
> Ethereal, as wee, or may at choice
> Here or in Heav'nly Paradises dwell.... (V. 497-500)

In Milton's refusal to specify any particular place as home for man, we have a position wholly consistent with the 17th-century's dissociation of sacredness from place. Yet so to acknowledge the ascendency of process—and of the belief that felicity inheres in person rather than in place—is not to conclude that paradise must eventually prove nothing more than a state of mind, or a trace in memory. Herrick, for one, was able to conceive even of a tomb as paradise if it proved to be the vessel of the divine presence. The truth is that for all the poets I have considered, lasting felicity—or "home"—involves transcendence, and not merely human inwardness.

I have argued throughout that, on the model of Eden's Garden, the paradisal in fact involves two modes of transcendence—the heavenly and the abyssal. To say this is not to adopt a philosophical dualism, since the primordial narratives invoked insist upon the inequality of these two modes, in authority as well as in function. And the contrasting categories, if carefully employed, do allow a conceiving of the paradisal in which both order and novelty obtain.

Yet neither of these modes of transcendence has prospered in the estimation of intellectuals since Milton's time. True enough, at the hands of Romantics like Blake and Shelley, the Deep became the realm of virtually all creative and redemptive energies.[23] And Wordsworth located in the mind of man a fathomless reach where the figures of Milton's angels and Jehovah appear as artifacts to be summarily dismissed.[24] But such positions have not arrested the drift away from belief in a transcendent Deep. Modern man appears content to take nature as a mysterious box of inexhaustible contents, with no compulsion to speak of a depth transcending the closed system of the empirical world. Furthermore, after the heavenly city of the 18th-century philosophers (as Carl Becker has described it[25]) faded into the light of common day, heaven—the other primary mode of transcendence—ceased to command the allegiance of the educated elite in the West.

The irony is that the dissociation of paradise from place, so brilliantly addressed by Milton and his contemporaries in imagery of idealized process —that is, of finitude rectified and consummated—should so soon become merely another tributary of the secularization identifying the modern age. If the sense of homelessness which pervades modern consciousness is a spiritual reflection of this secularization, we can scarcely expect any dramatic change in mood until the question of transcendence is re-opened. It seems likely that no age will prove more able than was Milton's to present the finite world, divorced from transcendence, as an adequate dwelling place for the human spirit.

NOTES

NOTES FOR THE INTRODUCTION

[1] See Chapter 6, "The Changing Nature of Utopian Assumptions," in her *Perfection and Progress: Two Modes of Utopian Thought* (Cambridge: The MIT Press, 1974).

[2] *A Treatise of Paradise* (London, 1617), pp. 7-8.

[3] Joseph Duncan provides a thorough review of the Renaissance discussions in *Milton's Earthly Paradise* (Minneapolis: The University of Minnesota Press, 1972), Chapter 6.

[4] *Paradise Lost* XI. 824-838. All references to Milton draw upon *Milton: Complete Poems and Major Prose*, ed. Merritt Y. Hughes (New York: The Odyssey Press, 1957). Hereafter references to *Paradise Lost* will appear in the text.

[5] *The Poems and Letters of Andrew Marvell*, ed. in two volumes by H. M. Margoliouth, second edition (Oxford: The Clarendon Press, 1952), I, 7.

NOTES FOR CHAPTER ONE

[1] It is possible that in the flight from Earth which Eve experiences in her Lucifer-inspired Dream, Milton means us to see yet another, albeit specious, version of the paradisal, which we might call Enlightened Finitude. The paradise of mystical flight, this is no true version, for it sidesteps the Fall, or to put the matter differently, it misdefines the Fall by identifying Fall and Creation. Felicity is achieved by fleeing the world. Eve tells how, when in her dream she had taken of the forbidden fruit:

> Forthwith up to the Clouds
> With him I flew, and underneath beheld
> The Earth outstretcht immense, a prospect wide
> And various: wondr'ing at my flight and change
> To this high exaltation; suddenly
> My Guide was gone, and I, methought, sunk down,
> And fell asleep.... (V. 86-92)

What Satan has promised Eve by way of wisdom and communion does not differ materially from what God at sundry other points in the poem promises man in the long run. But let us not miss Eve's final vantage point in the dream: "The Earch outstretcht immense, a prospect wide/And various...." Part of Milton's point is surely that Eve is precisely nowhere, with heaven unsecured, and the earth pointlessly remote. In the place of earth, or earth and heaven joined, she has the atmosphere, the realm of clouds, which is the seat of Satan and his minions in *Paradise Regained*. This yen to "see what life the Gods live," entailing as it does the flight from the earth, is to be condemned as a pernicious flight of fancy. Adam recognizes its source, and its peril.

2 Samuel Noah Kramer, *Sumerian Mythology*, rev. ed., Harper Torchbook (New York: Harper and Brothers, 1961), p. 55. This passage is drawn from the story of Enki and Ninhursag, the former of whom is the Sumerian water-god. Of course one does not need to go back five millennia for parallels. Mircea Eliade cites the contemporary myth told by the Brazilian tribe of Guaranis that paradise is a land without evil or work; see *The Quest: History and Meaning in Religion* (Chicago: The University of Chicago Press, 1969), pp. 107 ff.

3 Professor Klages shared these ideas in a public lecture given at the University of Illinois at Urbana-Champaign in the fall of 1972.

4 A. Bartlett Giamatti, it is true, in *The Earthly Paradise and the Renaissance Epic* (Princeton: The Princeton University Press, 1966), pp. 302-03, identifies a certain sluggishness attributed to Eden by Milton (cf. *PL*, IV. 237-40), but this does not materially alter the contrast Milton's Garden presents with the paradises described by antecedents like Beaumont and du Bartas.

Given the context of attitudes which I summarized in the Introduction, ought we not to ask, "Is it in fact Milton's intent that his readers see the inadequacies of the paradisal garden?" Or, phrased a bit differently: "Does Milton himself criticize his earthly paradise as finitude manqué?" If the question means "Does Milton mean for us to see the Garden as less than perfect?" the answer must surely be a negative. The description we find in Books IV and VIII is of an unflawed cynosure. Yet the prophecy of Milton's God which I cited as the opening of the present chapter testifies of a vision in which Edenic perfection is a point of departure rather than a terminus. In the Miltonic scheme there plainly are goods which lie beyond the Garden. To be honest with these evidences I attempt throughout to speak not of Milton's "criticism" of his Garden, but of the ways his story shows that Garden being transcended as the human career unfolds. One should speak, I suppose, not of the imperfections of Eden's Garden, but of its provisionality.

5 *The New Oxford Annotated Bible with the Apocrypha*, Revised Standard Version, edited by Herbert G. May and Bruce M. Metzger (New York: Oxford University Press, 1973), p. 3.

6 "Water," *The Interpreter's Dictionary of the Bible*, ed. George A. Buttrick (Nashville: The Abingdon Press, 1962), IV, 808.

7 Cf. Job 9:13; 26-5, 12-13; 38:16-17; 41:1-4; Psalms 17:5-6; 68:15-16; 74:13-14, 89:9-10; Isaiah 27:1.

8 Wensinck, *The Ocean in the Literature of the Western Semites* (Amsterdam: J. Müller, 1918), p. 65.

9 See Martz, *The Paradise Within* (New Haven: Yale University Press, 1964), especially his third chapter which is devoted to *Paradise Lost*, and Duncan, pp. 257-68. Here and in his compilation of 17th-century references to New Heaven and New Earth (pp. 242-57) Ducan is most helpful in researching the analogues to Milton in the poet's milieu. I believe it fair to add, however, that his interest is more taxonomic than polemic or thematic, and he does not explore the question of paradise's accommodation of process.

10 *Christian Doctrine*, ed. by Maurice Kelley and trans. by John Carey as Vol. VI in *The Complete Prose Works of John Milton* (New Haven: Yale University Press, 1973), p. 502.

11 *The Saint's Everlasting Rest* (London, 1650), pp. 44-45.

12 *The Christian* in *The Works of the Right Reverend Father in God Joseph Hall Lord Bishop of Norwich* (London, 1714), p. 338. I have found it convenient to use the folio collection of Hall's moral works for this and following references. The first edition of the complete works, prepared by the Rev. Josiah Pratt, did not appear until 1808.

13 *Works* (1714), p. 339.

14 *Calvin's Doctrine of the Christian Life* (London: Oliver and Boyd, 1959), p. 87. Wallace cites Calvin's commentaries on John 20:18 and Col. 3:1.

15 In another place (*The Pilgrim's Progress and Traditions in Puritan Meditation* [New Haven: Yale University Press, 1966]), I have shown how such heavenly-mindedness, as it was worked out in Puritan meditation, licensed the imagination in devotion and supplied a likely provenance for Bunyan's *The Pilgrim's Progress*.

16 *The Redemption of Bodies* in *The Complete Works of Richard Sibbes, D.D.*, ed. Alexander Grosart (Edinburgh, 1863), V, 166. Hereafter I refer to this collection as *Works*.

17 *Works*, IV, 292.

18 *Soliloquies: or, Holy Self-Conferences of the Devout Soul, Works* (1714), p. 231.

19 *A Breathing after God*, p. 157; *Light from Heaven* (London, 1638), p. 261. Thomas Taylor in his popular *The Parable of the Sower and the Seed* (London, 1621), pp. 384-85 draws out the same equation. (This last citation I owe to Duncan, pp. 260 and 313.)

20 *A Glance, Works*, IV, 167.

21 "Son-dayes," 1-5 and *passim* thereafter, in *The Works of Henry Vaughn*, ed. L. C. Martin, second edition (Oxford: The Clarendon Press, 1957), pp. 447-48.

22 Despite that recent trend in Milton readership, following upon Stanley Fish's *Surprised By Sin* (New York: St. Martin's Press, 1967), which presses to the limit the supposed Miltonic presumption of his reader's sinfulness, I would argue that Milton's boldness in presenting to us the

heavenly counsels, and the tonally troublesome divine statements, stems
from the conviction he shared with many of his time that regenerate man
might in this life enter confidently into the heavenly places, and might, in
his regeneracy, so fully identify with the divine point of view that the
qualifications introduced by sin were of minor consequence.

[23] *The Remedy of Prophaneness, Works* (1714), p. 205.

[24] Milton's imagery in this connection shows a striking likeness to the pictures
which open the masterpiece by his brilliant, if less erudite Puritan contemporary, John Bunyan. *The Pilgrim's Progress*, like *Paradise Regained*
a study of the regenerate life, begins with the narrator wandering in the
wilderness of this world. He comes upon a "Denn" where he sleeps and
dreams of a way to Celestial City. It is by the assurance of an utterly clear
and meaningful course that the wilderness of his waking experience is
transfigured.

It should be noted also that a century which began still honoring those
traditional and pessimistic tags about the stages of life which Jaques
mouths *In As You Like It* and which Samuel Chew has, in *The Pilgrimage of Life* (New Haven: Yale University Press, 1962), traced from the
Greeks forward, was by the time of Bunyan's *The Pilgrim's Progress*
(1678) prepared to acknowledge the individual career as progress both in
its older sense of journey and its modern figurative sense of meaningful
ascent. While not my concern here, it seems probable that in fact Bunyan's
allegory had a significant part in fixing the modern meaning. Certainly
there is keen irony in entertaining an Enlightenment optimism about the
individual career as a "progress" without any appreciation for the
heavenly-mindedness which in the 17th century gave that optimism a
spine.

[25] *Christian Doctrine, Works,* pp. 630 and 632.

[26] *Ibid.,* p. 620.

[27] For a wide-ranging discussion of this alteration in perspective, see Ms.
Nicolson's *The Breaking of the Circle* (New York: Columbia University
Press, 1960). Alexandre Koyré's *From the Closed World to the Infinite
Universe* (Baltimore: The Johns Hopkins Press, 1957) is particularly
concerned with the philosophical ramifications.

[28] *The Divine Poems of John Donne,* ed. Helen Gardner (Oxford: The
Clarendon Press, 1952), p. 30.

[29] *John Donne: The Anniversaries,* ed. Frank Manley (Baltimore: The
Johns Hopkins Press, 1963), p. 98.

[30] *A Preface to Paradise Lost* (Oxford: Oxford University Press, 1942), p.
81.

[31] *The Reason of Church Government, John Milton,* ed. M. Y. Hughes,
p. 643.

[32] *An Apology, The Student's Milton,* ed. Frank Allen Patterson, second
edition (New York: Appleton-Century-Crofts, 1933), p. 561.

[33] Milton is not alone in giving such high praise to the Long Parliament. Sir Henry Vane, in a speech against episcopal government (1641), claimed that the Long Parliament had been "called, continued, preserved, and secured by the immediate finger of God." Arthur Barker cites this remark in his *Milton and the Puritan Dilemma 1641-1660* (Toronto: The University of Toronto Press, 1942), p. 46.

[34] *Op cit.*, p. 632.

[35] *Saint's Everlasting Rest*, pp. 28 and 30. I include further references to this work in the text.

[36] This description appears in his Dedicatory Epistle (to Richard Hampden) in the 1670 reprinting of the work.

[37] Vaughan, *op. cit.*, p. 469. I quote the opening five lines.

[38] *Ibid.*, p. 476.

[39] *Works* (1714), p. 254.

NOTES FOR CHAPTER TWO

[1] In *Tenure*, Milton finds it "manifest that the power of kings and magistrates is nothing else but what is only derivative, transferred, and committed to them in trust from the people to the common good of them all, in whom the power yet remains fundamentally." Hughes, p. 755.

[2] *A Treatise on Angels* (London, 1613), p. 194.

[3] *Thomas Traherne: Centuries, Poems, and Thanksgivings*, ed. in two volumes by H. M. Margoliouth (Oxford: The Clarenden Press, 1958), I, 107.

[4] Hughes, p. 728.

[5] Cf. Seurat, *Milton: Man and Thinker* (New York: The Dial Press, 1928), pp. 123-26; Woodhouse, "Notes on Milton's Views on the Creation: The Initial Phases," *PQ*, 28 (1949), 211-236; Chambers, "Chaos in *Paradise Lost*," *JHI*, 24 (1963), 55-84.

[6] Robert M. Adams, "A Little Look into Chaos" in *Illustrious Evidence: Approaches to English Literature of the Early Seventeenth Century*, ed. Earl Miner (Berkeley: University of California Press, 1975). See particularly pages 86-89.

[7] Cf. Wensinck, *The Ocean in the Literature of the Western Semites*, p. 19.

[8] Milton was well versed in rabbinic materials, so it may not be irrelevant to cite the Talmudic argument, expounding Job 41:31, that indeed Eden was regularly visited by the monster of the deep:

> When Leviathan is hungry he emits [fiery] breath from his mouth and causes all the waters of the deep to boil; for it is said: *He maketh the deep to boil like a pot.* And if he were not to put his head into the Garden of Eden, no creature could stand his foul odor; for it is said: *He maketh the sea like a spiced broth.* (*Baba Bathra* in *The Babylonian Talmud* trans. into English under the editorship of

Rabbi Dr. I. Epstein [London: Soncino Press, 1935-1948], I, 298-299. The English translation of this section was made by Israel W. Slotki.)

The image of Leviathan's regular visits to Eden for the sake of prophylaxis is no whimsey, for we are assured that in this fashion "The sweet odours of the Garden of Eden perfume the sea." What is most notable here is the openness of paradise to the creature of flux, with the result that flux is itself altered.

[9] John Armstrong cites this passage in his argument for identifying Satan as the serpentine principle of flux. See *The Paradise Myth* (London: Oxford University Press, 1969), p. 106.

[10] Michael's review of holy history touches upon a number of crucial moments in the career of Israel, though the extent to which Milton meant them to fit the argument of his implicit theodicy I shall leave to the discernment of others.

[11] *Principalities and Powers in the New Testament* (Freiberg: Herder, 1961), pp. 60, 30-31.

[12] *The Evolution of the Dragon* (Manchester: The University Press, 1919), pp. 81-82.

[13] Cited by John Macquarrie in *God-talk: An Examination of the Language and Logic of Theology* (New York: Harper and Row, 1967), pp. 126-27. He is using the Greek text of *De Incarnatione*, xxv, 5-6, as translated by Archibald Robertson (London, 1891).

[14] Wensinck, p. 60.

NOTES FOR CHAPTER THREE

[1] *The Paradise Within*, pp. 3-31, 35.

[2] H. W. Swardson, *Poetry and the Fountain of Light* (London: Allen and Unwin, 1962), Chapter II; Cleanth Brooks, "What Does Poetry Communicate?" printed as Chapter Four in *The Well Wrought Urn* (New York: Harcourt, Brace and Co., 1947); cf. especially pp. 68-71 in the essay by Brooks.

[3] *The Poems of Robert Herrick* (Oxford, 1951), p. 370. I use the World's Classics reprinting of the F. W. Moorman text which in turn follows the 1648 edition. Page references I supply hereafter in the text.

Herrick's claustrophilia is not without precedents in medieval and Renaissance depictions of the womb. Imaginative empathy with the prenatal state certainly did not wait for the appearance of Freud. Sonnet 2 in Donne's La Corona sequence features the "deare wombe" of Mary in which the immensity of God was "cloystered" and Helen Gardner cites a number of precedents for Mary's womb as paradise, cloister, and bower. (See *The Divine Poems of John Donne* [Oxford: The Clarendon Press, 1952], pp. 59-60.) Jacob Boehme, we may suppose, was speaking something of a commonplace in observing that "Little Children are our Schoolmaster. . . . [T]hey bring their sport from the Mother's womb, which is a

Remnant of Paradise." (*Forty Questions on the Soul, The Works of Jacob Behman* gathered by William Law in four volumes (London, 1764), II, 100.

4 "At Play in the Garden of Ambivalence: Andrew Marvell and the Green World," *Criticism*, 17 (1975), pp. 295-307.

5 Geoffrey Hartman is, I believe, the first to apply the term "dialectical" to Marvell, and his reference is to the several pleasures the speaker entertains in "The Garden." He says, " 'The Garden,' as I see it, is dialectical rather than merely progressive in structure. It is true, but not all the truth, that the poet progresses from the vanities of the world to the pleasures of the garden, and finally to a garden within this garden—to the Eden which the soul is enabled to foresee in this, its earthly state." ("Marvell, St. Paul, and the Body of Hope," *Beyond Formalism* [New Haven: Yale University Press, 1970], pp. 169-70. This study originally appeared in *ELH*, 31 [1964]: 175-194.) In declaring that progression not to be all the truth, I take him to mean that the pleasures transcended are not simply left behind. Their partial values are to be incorporated into the final good, much as the promise of resurrection speaks to the preservation of bodily joys. "Dialectic" is in fact an indispensible term in discussing the whole of Marvell's poetic production.

6 Swan, p. 296.

7 This and all succeeding references to Marvell draw upon Margoliouth's edition cited in the Introduction, note 5. Hereafter I shall incorporate the line or stanza references into the text. The quotation above is from Margoliouth, I, 10, 23-24.

8 *A Late Discourse . . . Touching the Cure of Wounds by the Power of Sympathy* (London, 1658), p. 89.

9 This volume is one of four collected by James Winny in *The Frame of Order: An Outline of Elizabethan Belief Taken from Treatises of the Late Sixteenth Century* (London: Allen and Unwin, 1957). My reference is to p. 58.

10 Cf. Digby, *A Discourse Concerning the Vegetation of Plants* (London, 1661), pp. 39-40: "[T]he Sunne from without attracteth to the superficies of the fruit the most spiritful and aery parts of the ascending juyce."

11 "Upon the tree and stalk there groweth a *mixed* fruit, half earthly, and half according to the upper centre: and the fruit never cometh into a joy . . . unless it be satiated with the upper [part], and then it is ripe, for it hath attained Venus's body." Boehme, *The Threefold Life of Man* (London, 1650). I have used the 1909 reprinting of J. Sparrow's original English translation. The reference is to p. 305 in that reprint.

12 *Three Books of Occult Philosophy* (London, 1651), pp. 73-74.

13 *Plotinus: The Enneads*, trans. by Stephen MacKenna with that translation revised by B. S. Page (London: Faber and Faber, 1969), p. 380. In Plotinus' organization, the reference is to V.2.1.

[14] *The Philosophy of Plotinus* (London: Longmans Green and Co., 1918), I, 204.

[15] Inge, II, 147.

[16] *Paracelsus: Selected Writings*, ed. Jolande Jacobi and trans. by Norbert Guterman (London: Routledge and Kegan Paul, 1951), p. 119.

[17] It is symptomatic of the ambiguities in arguing from sources that the junction of soul, dew, and the water-cycle occur both in the early neo-Platonic discussions of the soul (G. R. Mead, apropos of quite another line of thought, points to Proclus and Porphyry) and in the profusion of tracts on occasional meditation. Cf. Mead's *The Doctrine of the Subtle Body in Western Tradition*, A Quest Book (Wheaton, Ill.: The Theosophical Publishing House, 1967), pp. 61-62, and Spurstow's *The Spiritual Chymist* (London, 1666), pp. 18-21.

[18] Cf. Ms. Wallerstein's *Studies in Seventeenth-Century Poetic* (Madison: The University of Wisconsin Press, 1950), Chapter Eight, and Kaufmann, *The Pilgrim's Progress and Traditions in Puritan Meditation*, pp. 170-87.

[19] "The Sinners Passing-Bell," *Works* (London, 1629), p. 252.

[20] Occasional meditation as we see it practiced in "Upon Appleton House" has a striking parallel in Thomas Vaughan's description of the "solid Christian philosopher" meditating in the out-of-doors:

> In the summer translate thyself to the fields, where all are green with the breath of God and fresh with the powers of heaven. Learn to refer all naturals to their spirituals by the way of secret analogy.... Sometimes thou mayst walk in groves, which being full of majesty will much advance the soul; sometimes by clear active rivers, for by such—say the mystic poets—is the way Apollo contemplated. ...This I would have thee walk in if thou dost intend to be a solid Christian philosopher. (*Anima Magica Abscondita* in *The Works of Thomas Vaughan*, ed. Arthur E. Waite [London: The Theosophical Publishing House, 1919], pp. 115-17.)

Granted, Marvell seems more often concerned to pose as "easie" than as "solid" philosopher, and there is in Marvell little if any of the esoteric elitism tinging this passage; yet the emphasis here upon the "powers of heaven" is consonant with Marvell's position.

[21] Louis Martz chooses to see Damon as addled with his love for Clorinda, so that this regard, rather than his careful deflecting of all attention to Pan-Christ earlier in the poem, becomes our final impression. Cf. *The Wit of Love* (Notre Dame: The University of Notre Dame Press, 1969), p. 157. Martz supposes that the "fearful religious question" of lines 15-16 is blunted at the close, with the threat to the pastoral world "gaily and humorously healed." But that is certainly to misjudge the power of the answer Damon himself offers to the threat. Gaiety and humor are by no means Marvell's only strategies for reconciling pastoral with the religious life.

For the text of the poem see Margoliouth, I, 18.

[22] See note *supra*.

[23] Consider the energy of Blake's Hell, or the role of Demogorgon as demiurge in Shelley's *Prometheus Unbound*. Northrop Frye has noted the Romantic inversion of the traditional cosmology: "Up" comes to designate the realm of despotic rule, indeed of all things evil; "Down" becomes the source of liberating good. Cf. *A Study of English Romanticism* (New York: Random House, 1968), pp. 23-26.

[24] See the preface to the 1814 edition of *The Excursion*.

[25] Carl L. Becker, *The Heavenly City of the Eighteenth-Century Philosophers* (New Haven: Yale University Press, 1932).